Contents

Smart Babies

A guide for identifying and supporting gifted traits in infants and young children

By Kathleen Casper, J.D.

Edited by Megan Lindale, Pediatric Nurse Practitioner

A handbook for parents, daycare providers, preschool teachers,

program administrators, medical providers, caseworkers,

and anyone else who cares for and about children

Smart Babies: A guide for identifying and supporting gifted traits in infants and young children

Edited by Megan Lindale

Cover photo from iStock by Getty Images

OneWorld Gifted, http://oneworldgifted.weebly.com

Kathleen Casper, J.D., Author

Kathleen is an educator and an attorney who is currently the president of the Florida Association for the Gifted (FLAG), as well as a gifted education consultant. She is the creator of the Casper Assessment for Social Emotional Skills (CASES) and an author on the OneWorld Gifted blog. She is the former national secretary of SENG (Supporting Emotional Needs of the Gifted), the Florida Department of Education's Gifted Education Specialist, the Washington Association for the Education of the Talented and Gifted president-elect, and the Tacoma Public Schools' Gifted Education Facilitator. She is also currently on the executive board of Florida's Pasco Hernando Early Learning Coalition and has an extensive history as an early learning educator and early learning center director. She is a foster parent as well as a parent of five gifted children. Kathleen is a child advocate and she presents nationally on gifted education issues.

Megan Lindale, ARNP, Editor

Megan is an Advanced Registered Nurse Practitioner with over twenty years of experience in the diagnosis, treatment, and follow-up of pediatric patients, ages birth through twenty-one years of age throughout the United States. She is also a certified school nurse who has provided school and public health services to children in preschool through high school, including gifted education and special needs programs for over a decade. As the parent and grandparent of gifted children, Megan is concerned about increasing support and knowledgeable care for gifted kids of all ages in the health and education systems.

1

Why we ALL should care about identifying and supporting gifted, young children

I had no idea that I should care about gifted issues until I was about 30 years old, even though I was in gifted programs myself as a child. I didn't understand that giftedness was much more than whether I, or other people, could perform well on academic tests. I didn't realize it was more than just labeling children so they could sit in different classes in the school system. And I certainly did not know then that understanding gifted issues was sometimes a life and death sort of thing. I didn't know that children were struggling with important social and emotional issues that could be better supported, if only I, and my friends and fellow community members knew more about those issues and what resources were available for these kids.

I hope that this book is one more tool to help more people start thinking about what giftedness really means. It is not merely a label. It is not something that screams "elitism" when you really know what it is (as many might think it does, because the way the word and designation have been used in the past and even currently, may be unfortunately twisted in order to promote that…). And it really does not mean "easier" children (as in, "teaching gifted kids must be easier…" or "gifted kids are easier to parent because they are so smart").

No, gifted children are not easier, nor are they always high performers. But they are definitely complex individuals who think in interesting ways, which can mean they possess intensities that can create wonderful pathways through life, or it can mean despair and constant hardship. There is a spectrum of possible gifted experiences, as there are a plethora of gifted traits and combinations of those traits that lead to so many different personalities and lives, that we cannot even start to tell you what "a gifted person is like." But we can discuss some of the things that gifted people may have in common, and we can talk about resources and strategies that can support them when things are tough and encourage them to reach for the stars with their unique abilities to tackle the world around them.

Community

This book is important for everyone. It doesn't matter whether you are a parent or a teacher, we all live in this world together. Just as we see people with other challenges in the world around us that have been labeled "disabilities," we also interact with people who are amazingly bright or who seem so different than we are, yet we just can't figure out what it is that makes them different. By understanding what gifted means, you can expand your own understanding of the community you live in. And many of you who pick up this book will also realize you or your family members or closest friends are likely gifted too, because often if you have a child who is gifted, others in the family are gifted as well. Gifted people are not always recognized as being gifted, or labeled officially as such, and gifted adults often don't have a clue that they are gifted—they may just think they are "weird," or they feel different from other people. So, if you are interested in more information, please see chapter 16, where I list many resources that you can use to learn more about the topic of giftedness across the lifespan and in adulthood too.

Parents

Parents often do not realize they have a gifted child until they are told they might have one. Usually that happens when their child is in school and is being compared with other children. Or it may be at the doctor's office when the child is making developmental gains at an unusual pace. Or they may just start wondering why their child is doing things that seem different than what their friends' children are doing. But all of these things usually occur when children are around preschool or elementary school age, which means that critical years are lost when parents could be supporting their babies' gifted characteristics and needs if only they knew about gifted issues earlier.

Parenting gifted children is difficult. Gifted children often struggle with asynchrony (having different rates of development in different areas, such as being highly advanced in their thinking skills, but still having young hands and struggling with motor skills; or having high abilities in acquiring knowledge in accelerated education areas, yet still acting like a very young child when interacting with other children their age, etc.). This means that as gifted children develop, they will hit many plateaus that are down-right frustrating and anxiety-producing. That, combined with their insatiable desire to learn and experience novel things, often pushes them into direct conflict with their caretakers who want to keep them safe and are in the role of supporters through the rough times. In other words, parenting gifted children can be exhausting and if parents are not aware of how normal this is for gifted children to be difficult, they may take it personally and struggle with their relationships with their children. So, the sooner parents of gifted children realize they are raising a gifted child, the better for everyone involved.

Relatives and friends

It is hard to raise gifted children without emotional support. Often that support comes from family and friends, so it makes sense that those people should understand your child's development and any unique traits. Many people do not know much about giftedness, so this gives you a great opportunity to share what you are learning about gifted education with them, so they can support you and your child as much as possible. If you are a friend or relative of someone who has a gifted child and you are reading this book, thank you for your wonderful support. Gifted children are often misunderstood and there are so many stereotypes about what gifted is. By you showing your interest in learning about gifted kids, you can help promote facts and helpful information with everyone you interact with too!

Daycare providers/Preschool teachers

Many children spend a lot of their time at daycare and/or preschool during their early years due to parents working or families desiring social interaction and educational practice for their children. Gifted children often benefit from learning experiences when the providers understand gifted traits and are able to support their unique learning and social-emotional needs.

Gifted children can have a lot of energy and need to constantly be interacting with new information or experiences. They usually are quick learners and don't need as much practice with new skills as other children. They advance through developmental stages at different speeds than others their age, and programs that are built based on the "average" child, may not work for them without flexibility in their placement.

Gifted infants and toddlers may start being mobile and verbal much earlier and become bored in "baby" rooms in daycares and preschools. They may need a lot of provider attention, which may be frustrating for the providers who are trying to meet the needs of multiple children. And they also may have difficulties interacting with the other children in the program, which may cause stress between the providers and parents as well.

Understanding possible gifted traits will enable providers to not only understand what children may need additional support during their academic development but will also give them more awareness of challenges the children may have, so as to better support their social-emotional needs and see those challenges as actual normal stages for gifted children rather than potential behavioral problems.

Program administrators

Administrators of daycare centers or preschool programs, or even administrators in local, state, or federal agencies that interact with/support young children should be aware of potential gifted traits so as to best support the kids in their care. It is important that our communities not only surround gifted children with understanding and support at the direct level, but that policies be created with awareness of gifted characteristics and needs as well. For an early learning program to work well for all children, those in administration and policy making/enforcement roles also need to understand what gifted children need.

Often programs are created with the "average" child in mind, meaning that they are age specific or based on developmental goals that children who fall in the middle of the ability bell curve can muster. However, programs that do not recognize the need for gifted children to interact with higher level challenges, or their need to sometimes access former lessons again because they did not master them along the same schedule or order that other children may have done, do not work well for gifted kids. In order to best support children who have gifted traits, programs and policies must be based on individualized needs (both academic and social-emotional), and should be flexible and based on supporting the whole child. This is a simplified list of requirements and the rest of this book will go into more specifics regarding potential issues, identifying characteristics and needs, and strategies that will help administrators more fully understand giftedness in infants and young children so they can create and support programs that work better for all kids.

If you are reading this and you know an education program administrator, please pass this book along to them too, and if you are an administrator, thank you for being an advocate for gifted children!

Medical providers

A major concern that parents of gifted young children have is that they want to find medical providers who also understand their children. Many gifted youths have special needs that require specialized medical care, including sensitivities, allergies, mental health issues and more. If a medical provider is unaware of gifted traits, they may misdiagnose the child or at least miss part of the situation (please see the information on misdiagnosis in the resource section). Gifted children may also be twice exceptional, meaning that they have additional challenges than giftedness only, and that means even more potential medical implications.

Medical providers (and this includes dental, mental health, pediatricians, specialists, and more) are not always up to date on gifted education or the latest research on gifted issues, so hopefully this book will help them be more aware and be prepared to share information on local, state and national resources for parents. Medical providers may also be some of the first to notice gifted traits regarding a child's development in comparison with other children. And they are in a unique position of trust that can provide parents with peace of mind when the going gets tough.

Caseworkers, judges, lawyers and others in the court and juvenile justice system

There are foster children who are gifted, as well as children in juvenile criminal court systems that are gifted. One might even guess that this also means that there are gifted children in parts of the court system who may be under-identified as gifted as well.

This means that those who work with children in the system should also be aware of gifted traits and how they can impact the children.

Gifted infants often also may have gifted parents, which means that whole families may be in need of specialized support. In order to keep families together and work with them through depression, anxiety, and other issues that are common when a family member is involved in the court system, those involved should understand the intense social emotional reactions that gifted people may also exhibit. Also, when monitoring child development in order to keep tabs on child welfare issues, it is important to understand the unique attributes and possible asynchronous development of gifted babies and children. Understanding gifted issues is as important as understanding potential disability issues.

Why we need to keep learning even more about giftedness

The reasons listed above describe many reasons why specific people should be interested in understanding potential gifted traits and related needs of gifted children, but a brief awareness is often not enough. People are complex and giftedness is present in all areas of a gifted person's life. And it's not enough to learn about common characteristics, because gifted people can be so different. As I've heard this often said, "If you've met one gifted person, you've met ONE gifted person." It is important that we all keep up on the research and that we apply what we know to each gifted person, individually.

The rest of this book will cover the following topics that should be helpful for anyone who works with or is raising a potentially gifted baby or young child. After reading this book, the goal is that you could identify possible gifted traits in infants, toddlers, preschoolers and young school aged children; recognize biases and misunderstandings and apply strategies to support young children who are gifted. And if all else fails, there are several resources and experts in the field who are happy to help continue this conversation and you can find more information about how to get involved and contact those resources in the final chapter.

My Local Resources and Gifted Education Experts, Resources, etc.

People or other resources I can contact for information about gifted education issues in my community, state, country, world:	Email addresses, phone numbers, websites, and other contact information for my gifted team members:	Notes:

2

Giftedness in general

There are many books on the market about gifted children. This is not a replacement for them, but rather an addition, as this book focuses more specifically on potential gifted traits in infants and very young children. But it is important to also understand some of the issues surrounding giftedness in the rest of the community too.

Identification issues

The term gifted is defined in several different ways, but most states require a school aged child to be able to show talent in academics, and/or a high intellectual quotient (IQ) of usually around 130 points or higher in order to be considered gifted for the sake of getting public school gifted services.

Schools often use achievement to measure high abilities, and call those who can achieve at high levels compared with others in their age groups, gifted, (for example, see the Los Angeles Unified School District's criteria for "gifted in the high achievement category," at http://achieve.lausd.net/Page/1997). Others recognize creativity and/or success in the arts as a necessary attribute of giftedness, and others add even more possible avenues for identification (see all the different state education system definitions at the National Association for Gifted Children, NAGC's site: http://www.nagc.org/sites/default/files/Advocacy/State%20definitions%20%288-1-13%29.pdf).

These methods of identification are not without critics. Research shows that using IQ to determine giftedness leaves out many different children, especially those in populations that have historically been under-identified (those who are non-Caucasian, and those who are from low income homes or are English language learners). There are some tests that are touted as being more culturally sensitive and potentially identifying more students by using nonverbal methods (such as the Naglieri Nonverbal Ability Test, or NNAT). And there are several states that allow for other means than using an IQ score as a gate-keeping mechanism, such as using portfolios, rating scales showing gifted characteristics, and more.

What all of these definitions and requirements do not deal with, is how to identify and support gifted children BEFORE they go to school. What do we do with gifted children when they are making their largest gains in development that they will make during the course of their whole lives, during their birth through age 5 years? In order to define giftedness at pre-elementary-school ages, we need to discuss what giftedness really means as a whole, not just in terms of school or academics.

It's important that even if we use the national or state public education definitions, that we focus on the words that allow for more than just merely high performers in academics to be recognized. The NAGC position paper on "Definitions of Giftedness" (http://www.nagc.org/resources-publications/resources/definitions-giftedness) states that "We assert that there are children who demonstrate high performance, or who have the potential to do so," and they go on to say, "we have a responsibility to provide optimal educational experiences to fully develop talents in as many children as possible, for the benefit of the individual and the community."

The NAGC statement above implies that children do not have to be high performers in order to be gifted, but it does focus on developing talents. However, history has shown that there are many gifted people who do not grow up to have extraordinary talents—many gifted people lead relatively average lives and never are seen as high performers, and that is just fine!

As stated in the abstract of a presentation by Abdul Latif from Grand Valley State University in Michigan, (from his presentation titled, "Analysis of Childhoods of William James, Teddy Roosevelt, Rabindranath Tagore, and Jawaharlal Nehru," at http://files.eric.ed.gov/fulltext/ED400663.pdf),

> "It is difficult to ascertain what factors in childhood help achieve greatness in adulthood and beyond. Plato recognized that many famous parents often raised ordinary or even infamous children. On the other hand, countless

individuals who made remarkable contributions to art, literature, science, medicine, and politics often came out of adverse or hostile personal circumstances. Also, many did not have formal education, or at least, not in the domain in which they demonstrated unusual gifts."

Most importantly, gifted people need to grow up and have the freedom to do whatever it is that they are compelled to do, and we can do what we can to help them get there by providing them, and those who care for them when they are young, with information and support about gifted characteristics and needs. Then they can be understood and understand themselves, regardless of what they end up doing for jobs in their futures.

Dr. Subotnek et al. (2011) came up with a framework of looking at giftedness that includes the whole child and acknowledges that without appropriate supports, gifted people cannot effectively harness their potential. They explained giftedness as:

"a developmental process that *is domain specific and malleable*. Although the path to outstanding performance

may begin with demonstrated potential, *giftedness must be developed and sustained by way of training and interventions in domain-specific skills, the acquisition of the psychological and social skills needed to pursue difficult new paths, and the individual's conscious decision to engage fully in a domain. The goal of this developmental process is to transform potential talent during youth into outstanding performance and innovation in adulthood."* (http://journals.sagepub.com/stoken/rbtfl//bwNip9GMWEg2/full)

This definition is pointedly focused on performance as the main goal in identifying and supporting these gifted people. But it is noteworthy because of the heavy reliance on the mission of acquiring skills in order to manifest the greatest abilities of the individual. A gifted person does not have to perform, but if we want to provide our gifted children with the opportunities to do well in the things they choose to do in life, we can use this definition as an inspiration to support them with domain-specific skills as well as psychological and social skills, so as to support the whole child.

The most critical time to identify and support gifted children is when they are really young and are starting to establish their relationships and beliefs about learning, and while they are developing their skills from the very beginning of their lives.

Misconceptions

So many people believe that gifted is the same thing as being talented. Or that gifted means the same as high achiever. There is a lack of understanding about the overwhelmingness of being gifted—that people who are gifted, ARE gifted. They don't have to behave certain ways or produce anything extraordinary in order to be gifted. Their brains are wired in ways that promote learning and help them think deeply about issues, but whether or not they use them to jump through the hoops of educational programs in ways that astound people with excellence is up to them.

Some gifted people perform well in school, and some gifted people do not. Some are great at math, and some at language arts. Some are great at anything they put their minds to, and some have such anxiety and possibly other barrier behaviors or responses to education that they refuse to perform well at all. Some have learning disabilities and are considered twice exceptional (or 2e), and some have disabilities that are never considered because they hide them under their abilities to achieve just well enough so that no one ever suspects anything could be wrong.

Sometimes the fact that gifted has been equated with high performance hinders the entire profession of gifted education because the elitism that is created by using a label to imply that some children will perform better than others means that others with actual gifted traits that do not perform well are not supported well, or even at all in some areas. Children with gifted traits are not elite, they are children. They may choose to focus their efforts on schoolwork, like other children may do. Or they may not. But all children with gifted traits are valuable and need support, just as all children need support. Some may need support to deal with issues caused by their giftedness, and some may not need support and do just fine. What they all need though, is to be surrounded by caring teachers, parents, and others who understand the potential problems that giftedness could cause. That way, if there are any negative behaviors or other social-emotional issues, the team of educators and others can help the child through them and not judge the child unfairly without keeping the gifted traits and needs in mind.

Gifted traits

There are some good lists out there that include traits that many gifted people have. However, not every gifted person has every trait, and they all have different combinations.

Most gifted people do have a tendency to have the following traits though, as shown in the following chart (in comparison with people who are not gifted, but who are bright and can perform well in school) —

BRIGHT CHILD

- Knows the answers
- Is interested
- Is attentive
- Has good ideas
- Works hard
- Answers the questions
- Top group
- Listens with interest
- Learns with ease
- 6-8 repetitions for mastery
- Understands ideas
- Enjoys peers
- Grasps the meaning
- Completes assignments
- Is receptive
- Copies accurately
- Enjoys school
- Absorbs information
- Technician
- Good memorizer
- Enjoys straightforward, sequential presentation
- Is alert
- Is pleased with own learning

GIFTED LEARNER

- Asks the questions
- Is highly curious
- Is mentally and physically involved
- Has wild, silly ideas
- Plays around, yet tests well
- Discusses in detail, elaborates
- Beyond the group
- Shows strong feelings and opinions
- Already knows
- 1-2 repetitions for mastery
- Constructs abstractions
- Prefers adults
- Draws inferences
- Initiates projects
- Is intense
- Creates a new design
- Enjoys learning
- Manipulates information
- Inventor
- Good guesser
- Thrives on complexity
- Is keenly observant
- Is highly self-critical

(From Challenge Magazine by Good Apple, 1989)

Gifted adults and school-aged children often have specific needs that correspond with their gifted characteristics. I created the following chart to explain some of those needs in a nutshell, below.

Possible Gifted Characteristics	Related Needs:
Enjoys learning, is curious, observant, asks many questions, observant, reflective, moves from interest to interest, quick learners, voraciously devours information when excited or curious about the topic	New and novel ideas, based on topics that the child is interested in Inquiry projects that are open-ended or provide for multiple avenues for exploration interest-driven activities that have at least some problem-solving or new skill acquisition involved Few time limits Projects or discussions that promote complex thought processes
Focused on fairness and justice, emotionally sensitive, looks for the "big picture" first and then breaks it down into parts to understand the world and related issues	Outlets for expressing emotional responses to current or historical events and room to fall apart as needed Opportunities to contribute to the world around them and projects that promote connections with the greater community Information about issues that are not fair, or instances of injustice so they can understand more about the issues Opportunities for debate or sharing ideas about current events Role models or other leaders to guide the child or to discuss issues
Inventive, creative, enjoys sensory things (or may need things a particular way because of sensory overload), psychomotor intensities (may need to move often or may have ticks or other repetitive movements), imaginative, more aware of colors/lighting/sounds	Opportunities for the hands-on manipulation of materials into new or better things A safe environment to move their body and be active Freedom to have new ideas and try out new concepts Encouragement and patience with wild and silly ideas Bravery to fail multiple times before they succeed with a new idea
Struggles with finding like-interest/intellectual peers, overly talkative/expressive, focused intensely on topics of interest, issues with communicating effectively (controlling intense emotions in their response to circumstances, discussing things that they find easier to understand than others do, etc.)	Time with other like-minded individuals of multiple ages Role modeling and practice with social-emotional skills A safe environment to make mistakes and learn from them Practice with executive functions Self-awareness and understanding of gifted traits Support from others who understand their intensities and accept them while they struggle through social-emotional growth

There are interesting findings in the area of brain research regarding giftedness.

According to Mrazik and Dombrowski (2010), in The Neurobiological Foundations of Giftedness, Researcher Winner (2000), there are five trends often noted among gifted children:

> First, children who are gifted in math, the arts, and music demonstrate enhanced right-brain activity compared to normal children on tasks specific to the right hemisphere.

> Second, gifted children are disproportionately not right-handed.

> Third, musically and mathematically gifted children have more bilateral, symmetrical brain organization where the right hemisphere appears to be more involved in tasks ordinarily reserved for the left hemisphere.

> Fourth, giftedness in spatial activities is accompanied by a disproportionate incidence of language-related disorders including dyslexia.

Fifth, children with higher IQs have a higher incidence of autoimmune problems and myopia.

Mrazik and Dombrowski (2010) also mention that gifted people have a unique "capacity to persevere on tasks and repetitively improve and enhance their ability well beyond what others typically do," and they believe that giftedness occurs or is emphasized due to prenatal exposure to excess hormones, such as testosterone, which then affects the formation of the brain and patterns of information networking in the brain hemispheres to allow for this advanced cognitive ability. Other researchers have found that the prenatal period (including chemical exposures, stress, depression, drug and alcohol use and nutrition), has a huge impact on IQ, measures of neural conduction speed, and tests of cognitive ability (see Annie Murphy Paul, Origins, at *http://anniemurphypaul.com/books/origins-how-the-nine-months-before-birth-shape-the-rest-of-our-lives/*).

There are also environmental factors that influence whether gifted children are able to develop talents that would allow them to be identified for services (poverty, racial biases, trauma, etc.). And there are books and articles about how gifted children can improve their abilities using mindset techniques. (See Carol Dweck,

Mindset: The New Psychology of Success (2007). And for more

discussion on the topic that is specific to gifted children, see

Raising Gifted Kids: Carol S. Dweck on the Impact of Mind-set, at

http://highability.org/83/carol-s-dweck-on-the-impact-of-mind-set/.)

Researchers disagree on whether a gifted is "not what you do, it's

who you are" (Dr. Jim Delisle, http://old.post-

gazette.com/regionstate/20010610giftediqsidereg8.asp), or if it is

what you do, not who you are (Slobotnik et al., 2011). But gifted

expert Annemarie Roeper believed that giftedness went deeper

than all of that and is based on an intrinsic core difference:

It is my belief that the gifted child is emotionally different

from others. The Self of the gifted child is structured

differently. The depth of their awareness is different. The

center of their inner life is different. Their view of the world is

more complex in a fundamental way. That is why one cannot

say the child is "partially gifted" in certain areas only and not

in others. (Roeper A. (1996). A personal statement of

philosophy of George and AnneMarie Roeper. Roeper

Review, 19, 18-19)

This belief is evident in the many lists of potential characteristics

that experts have found that gifted people often have, due to their

unique brains and advanced learning abilities and experiences. The

main things that we should keep in mind about gifted characteristics

and needs are the following:

- **Gifted Characteristics are not just academic, and**

- **Gifted Characteristics can be considered negative or**

   positive, depending on the situation.

Most gifted traits have to do with the social-emotional growth of the

child, and how they interact with their environment around them.

Some of the characteristics of gifted children make it easier for

them to learn, but some of those characteristics can also make it

harder for them to learn. It depends on how they are allowed to

interact with information and explore the concepts, and it depends

on who is supporting that learning, and whether it is being

"crammed down their throats," or if they are chasing the information themselves out of their own interests or curiosity. It also depends on who is along for the journey, and how well they are respected and honestly liked, so that they are able to struggle through the hard parts in a safe and supportive place.

The "Ups and Downs of Giftedness" chart by Dr. James T. Webb also shows the dichotomy of giftedness, and how the same gifted traits can be seen as both positive and negative. It is found in the book Helping Gifted Children Soar, 2nd edition, and at www.greatpotentialpress.com/living-with-the-ups-and-downs.

I compiled this checklist (below) that educators and parents can use to determine whether a child is in need of a gifted evaluation and/or possibly acceleration (and in order to help educators and parents keep in mind that the child may have asynchronous traits that may otherwise impact their kindergarten readiness evaluation and may appear as if the child was not mature enough for kindergarten). I share it here and encourage you to think about other characteristics that make gifted children unique and in need of alternate experiences compared with their nongifted peers.

Does the child exhibit any of the following traits?

-the child prefers to socialize with the teacher rather than students in their age range

-the child has a high level of knowledge about an issue or thing that he or she is personally interested in

-the child has a high level of vocabulary

-the child does not seem to know how to effectively engage other students in socialization activities such as working with others, sharing information, joking around, etc.

-the child is uninterested in what students their age are doing, but may be more interested in helping younger children or engaging with much older people.

-the child is much more interested in the big picture or asks many "why" and "how" questions about the way things work or fit into the world in a larger scale.

-the child seems knowledgeable about things happening in the world outside school or is very interested in social or justice issues if they are told about them.

-the child has a lot of energy and/or can be easily distracted by something that is more interesting than the lesson in class.

-the child is highly sensitive to sensory stimulation—such as smells, bright lights, loud noises, itchy clothing, bumps in their socks, etc.

-the child has a high level sense of humor.

-the child seems to enjoy arguing or finding exceptions to rules or statements.

-the child seems to constantly be challenging authority or boundaries.

-the child seems to not have common sense when it comes to "street smarts" (paying attention to safety issues or social issues), but seems highly intelligent or attentive in areas of personal interest (asynchronous development).

-the child shows perfectionist traits.

-the child has extreme highs and lows and seems emotionally intense (seeming to overreact to emotional stimulation).

-the child seems anxious about things even more than other children his or her age in similar situations, such as worrying about being safe in a plane if they are traveling soon, or worrying about the safety of a parent when they aren't together, or worrying about their own performance, etc.

If a child exhibits these types of behaviors they may be gifted traits and not maturity issues. It is important that the child be screened further for a need for gifted support services, and the earlier they are given access to support, the better. Gifted students should not be screened out of academic acceleration due to gifted traits that they may never "grow out of."

(http://oneworldgifted.weebly.com/blog/gifted-kids-and-early-entrance-to-kindergarten)

Gifted Education Issues and Questions

Record your questions or notes here:

3

Biases and misunderstandings

One of the things I do when I present trainings to educators and others about gifted characteristics is I give them a sheet with tons of different general characteristics listed on it. I ask the participants to do the following:

- Independently circle gifted characteristics on the page

- Get with tablemates to discuss gifted characteristics—what is circled, and why?

Then I watch as some of them circle assorted words throughout the page, often picking words that have to do with misconceptions of "gifted meaning high performing" or being well-behaved. A few people will see through my assignment and sit back and giggle to themselves because they can see what I am trying to do—my point is to show that often people believe the misconceptions and don't realize that gifted children have a multitude of characteristics.

There are several traits that are more likely to be found in gifted people—those traits listed in the previous chapter, but gifted children are kids, so they also have other traits too. Those who understand what gifted means, know that gifted kids can have all sorts of traits. This activity allows us to talk honestly about the misconceptions that some participants have and start to deconstruct them.

Misconceptions and myths about giftedness

There are a lot of misconceptions out there. The NAGC states several myths about gifted children in their position paper titled "Myths about Gifted Students," including:

- Gifted Students Don't Need Help; They'll Do Fine on Their Own
- Gifted Kids Will Be Fine in The Regular Classroom

- Gifted Students Make Everyone Else in The Class Smarter by Providing A Role Model or A Challenge

- All Children Are Gifted

- Gifted Education Programs Are Elitist

- That Student Can't Be Gifted, He Is Receiving Poor Grades

- Gifted Students Are Happy, Popular, And Well Adjusted in School

- Our District Has a Gifted and Talented Program: We Have AP Courses

- Gifted Education Requires an Abundance of Resources

They also discuss issues such as acceleration and twice exceptional issues. To read the discussions on each of these myths, please see their paper at: *http://www.nagc.org/resources-publications/resources/myths-about-gifted-students*.

Gifted education specialist, Dr. Carolyn Coil, also lists some similar myths as well as others that have more to do with the whole child and not just about academic performance in her article she wrote for CNN's Schools of Thought website, titled "My view: Ten myths about gifted students and programs for gifted." Dr. Coil discusses many issues, including the following: a discussion regarding the need for additional gifted services because gifted children can do even better in school with support; the problem of using IQ and achievement to identify giftedness; the need for early identification of gifted children; stereotypes about what gifted children look or act like; that gifted children do not always behave wonderfully or achieve at high levels, and more. I did not list the myths here, so if you want to read more about the myths and the discussion about each, please see her article at

http://schoolsofthought.blogs.cnn.com/2012/11/14/ten-myths-about-gifted-students-and-programs-for-gifted/.

Risk factors impacting many gifted children

Once we dispel the myths that people in our community believe about giftedness, then we need to also recognize and understand the different types of risks that may impact whether gifted children are identified at all. Unfortunately, the school system often only is able to pick up students who stand out as being "exceptional" in terms of high or low level academic success. Those students who are meeting expectations, but who may not be excelling may not be flagged at all for gifted evaluation. And those who are low-performing may be more likely to be evaluated for special education services for potential remedial support than to be evaluated for gifted services, even when their gaps in learning are due to (or even partially due to) their gifted traits. This is important to think about because it is hard enough to get average performers gifted support in the school system, but twice exceptional learners are even less likely to be identified.

It is also important to think about what underperformance means when we are thinking about gifted children who have high potential. Underperformance is usually defined as performing lower than what someone is able to do. But gifted children usually have high potential to succeed under ideal situations, and yet they are often compared with other children their age who are not gifted. So, a gifted child who is not working to their highest potential, still may seem to be performing just "fine." So, they may not be flagged as needing additional support.

It is also important to keep in mind that there are many types of life situations that may create underperformance in gifted children. When a child is experiencing challenges in their home, or they are facing biases in the community, they may not perform well during formal gifted evaluations. And sometimes these at-risk situations are less than obvious.

Youth can become at-risk for many different reasons and may respond in different ways to the stress caused by the following:

- POVERTY
- RACE/CULTURAL ISSUES
- TRAUMA
- SOCIAL & EMOTIONAL NEEDS
- MISDIAGNOSIS
- TWICE EXCEPTIONALITY

We will look at each of these issues separately below, but keep in mind that many children have more than one of these situations going on at the same time. For example, a child in poverty may also be of a race that is historically not identified as often for gifted support services; or a child who has been in trauma may also suffer from bullying or other social issues. In other words, we need to be cognizant of the potential at-risk factors and be alert to combinations of them as well.

Sometimes those risk factors will be masked by the ability of the child to pretend that everything is ok. Many gifted children who are underperforming will skate along at the C-average level in school, or act as normal as possible, due to a fear that they will be discovered and someone might make them feel like they are even more different from their like-age peers as they already feel. So, while we are looking for risk factors and want to help gifted kids who otherwise may not be identified or well-served, we do need to be careful not to make them feel that they are different than the crowd in ways that may impact their social status or self-esteem as we proceed. This goes for even young children, who do not want to have to do anything different than the other kids if it seems scary or they aren't sure what you are trying to do. So, any approach to support them should be as normalized as possible—for example, working with the parents so that the child knows the parents support what you are doing, and talking with them during the course of playing or doing something that they do every day.

Poverty

Children who live in low income homes are often at a disadvantage when they come into school if they have not had as many extracurricular experiences as other students, or if they have not been surrounded by the same learning materials, such as books and other toys that promote fine and large motor skills that lead to success in reading and early math concepts. This disadvantage can be alleviated by having parents or caregivers that still prioritize learning activities such as reading library books to their children or taking them to free community events that provide experiences similar to those that other families may pay for, such as community open houses at art workshops, museums, science centers, or other hands-on types of organizations. Free or reduced preschool activities also can help promote early learning, and many communities now offer at least some services for preschoolers or young children who have learning concerns (which can be helpful for our twice exceptional students).

Children from low income families are unfortunately less likely to be identified formally for gifted services when they are in school (http://www.davidsongifted.org/Search-Database/entry/A10670), and may have parents who are less able to advocate for services because they may be working during school hours, or they may not be as aware of the possible avenues for advocacy if they do not feel empowered with enough information. They also may not be part of the community of parents who pass on the information about how to promote their children's educational needs. Sometimes educational experiences go to those who ask, and not everyone knows the same amount of information, unfortunately.

It's important for all parents and caregivers to be aware of their options for their child's learning. School districts, preschools and daycares, as well as medical providers and other community members should do what they can to ensure that information is equitably dispersed. This does not always happen as well as it should though, and parents who are not available to attend as many school or community events, or who do not talk as much with the other parents who do hold the information are at a distinct disadvantage.

Parents of all socio-economic statuses (SES) need to do whatever they can to ensure that their children are exposed to reading at young ages and that they have opportunities to expand their vocabulary. Some community members expose their children to specific vocabulary through travel and visiting new locations such as zoos and museums, so even if a family does not have a lot of extra money for extra things, finding ways to access those same discussions is important—such as watching videos on different types of adventures or travel, reading books about foreign places, or taking walks in the community so you can talk about new concepts and words.

Children who live in low income areas may also be zoned for schools that are underperforming and struggle to attract teachers. They may be exposed to environments that detract from their abilities to focus on education, and they may come from homes that do not value education as much as others. It is clear that low SES can impact the success of students, but it is not always the case and there are ways to counteract those environmental influences. However, we need to keep in mind that there is usually not an even playing field, and gifted children from low SES homes may not be as easily identified through traditional gifted evaluations as other children are. This is a huge reason that we need to promote identification and support for gifted children in the earliest years of their lives so we can provide them with the support they need as early as possible.

Race and cultural issues

The United States has done a poor job, overall at identifying our diverse gifted children. Most gifted programs identify more white children than non-white children and historically the Native, Black, and Hispanic/Latino/a populations are seriously under-represented in K-12 gifted programs. This is an issue that stems from biases and inadequate and inequitable identification policies. Children of color who are gifted are not always given a fair shot by IQ testing or academic achievement tests for a variety of reasons—first of all, the tests themselves are controversial, with many education experts claiming they are overtly discriminatory; and racially diverse children are not referred for testing as much as Caucasian children (see Dr. Donna Ford, et al.'s article at http://files.eric.ed.gov/fulltext/ED505479.pdf),

Even when Native, Black, and Hispanic children are identified for gifted services, the services may not be sufficient to meet the needs of diverse students and the children may end up choosing not to participate. For example, many gifted programs are housed in schools that many other schools feed into by bussing the gifted students to the program location, which is not supportive of the cultural ties that the children often have to their neighborhoods. Sometimes the programs require parent participation and parents are unable to drive across town to participate or they (and the children) feel like they do not fit in when most of the children in the program are different races than their own.

Teachers need to be culturally competent in order to ensure that the programs support all children, including all races and they need to reach out to families in order to make sure everyone feels welcome and can participate. It is also recommended that programs be housed in children's home schools and that services be provided as an integrated service that occurs throughout the days by trained teachers, rather than for a limited time outside of the normal school program so the students have constant support and can continue to participate with their friends and neighbors. Parents who are concerned about these issues should ask questions and be willing to advocate for their children's individual needs so that the programs provide what they need, which can be stressful for families at times and could add to the hardships of trying to find the right services and support for intense children.

It is important that educators not assume that students from diverse racial backgrounds are automatically at a disadvantage in terms of achievement or educational attainment. As Hughes and McGee (2010) point out, "students from nonmainstream cultures and languages have different educational and cultural experiences: in contrast, students from poverty have restricted experiences. If poverty and cultural differences are combined, it is the restricted nature of different experiences that can lead to a serious and significant loss of academic achievement" (chapter 8: Educational systems in the identification and development of high ability in infants through grade 3, Hughes and McGee, from Special Populations in Gifted Education: understanding our most able Students from Diverse Backgrounds, Sourcebooks, Inc.).

Infants and very young children may not have as many of these issues yet, due to not yet being in the public-school system. But they may have parents who are dealing with some of the issues that come from biases and inequities in the community. Some communities are segregated and community services can be of lower quality or harder for families to access and children may not have access to as many opportunities for screenings or other pre-school services. Parents of Native, Hispanic and Black children should learn what they can about gifted issues as early as possible and get as involved as possible so they can be a part of the solutions to these types of issues in their communities, or at least be aware of programmatic differences before their young children are school aged.

There are a few very strong multicultural gifted education advocates who share their experiences of overcoming hardships and who have well-regarded reading materials available for families who want more information about race/diversity issues. Parents who are interested in networking with these experts can access them for discussions at state and national gifted education conferences.

Trauma

Students who have had experiences in their lives that caused them emotional pain, such as experiencing domestic violence in the home, abuse or neglect, a death in the family or an extended or sudden serious illness, drug or alcohol addiction of family members, or other intense challenges may be under the effects of trauma. Children experiencing trauma are unable to focus on learning and need to have their immediate safety needs met before they can get back to the education process. This means that they are more concerned about what is going on at home, or the losses they have suffered (be it losses of relationships, trust, etc.), and they need to get through that immediate (and often long-lasting) trauma before they can move on.

Research has shown that trauma adversely affects the ability to acquire communication skills, understand cause and effect, take the perspective of others, focus on instruction, regulate their emotions, engage in lessons, organize their time and materials and follow rules (The Heart of Learning & Teaching Compassion, Resiliency and Academic Success, Wolpow et al., 2009).

According to research, the behaviors of children experiencing emotional pain can look like misbehavior such as "disrespect, disobedience, willfulness, moodiness, excessive anger, not being able to sit still, and a whole host of behaviors..."
(*http://www.acesconnection.com/blog/school-troubled-kids-trauma-the-brain-and-pain-based-behaviors*).

It is important that caretakers and providers of gifted children who have experienced trauma be aware of the effects of trauma and understand that these children may be even more at-risk of depression, anxiety and other social-emotional stresses due to their added layer of gifted traits. Gifted children often experience emotional stimuli even more intensely than others do, and they have innate cravings for justice and peace that may make them feel even more responsible for making everyone around them feel better and they may take on the worries of others more than they should.

Infants and young children also experience the effects of trauma and their cognitive development can also be impacted. It is important that caretakers of young children be aware of the issues surrounding trauma in young children and be on the lookout for those effects when they know the children have experienced emotional events in their young lives.

All that being said, experiencing trauma or having a difficult childhood does not mean a child is unlikely to be gifted or to excel after they deal with the immediate traumatic experience. In fact, many eminent people in the history of our world have had traumatic childhoods and have used those experiences to motivate them towards further achievement. As Subotnik et al. (2011) states, "It has been suggested that these environments facilitate creative productivity by engendering characteristics that help individuals meet the demands of creative careers or jobs that involve tackling ill-defined, unstructured, and complex problems. These characteristics include early psychological independence, self-sufficiency, an ability to cope with high levels of stress, resiliency, emotional strength, a tolerance for ambiguity, intellectual risk taking, and a preference for challenge. Difficult childhoods, childhood trauma, or experiences of marginalization may also create compelling psychological needs that are ameliorated or compensated for through creative productivity in adulthood."

(http://journals.sagepub.com/stoken/rbtfl//bwNip9GMWEg2/full)

Social emotional needs

Young children may experience hardships with social and emotional skills. The asynchrony of gifted development means that children who seem older than they really are, may still act younger at times and often that occurs with bright children reverting to very young behaviors when caretakers least expect it. Some children do not master the social emotional skills that are needed when they are in public situations and those challenges will give them trouble for many years into their futures.

It is important that gifted children be given the support they need in order to learn coping skills for dealing with both other gifted people in their lives, as well as others who are not gifted. Some parents choose to keep their bright kids in situations where they will only be exposed to other children of similar intellectual abilities, but this limits their practice with working with others and may make it harder for them to adapt to heterogenous groups in the future. Some parents isolate their young children so much that they have difficulties working with other bright children too, so that they do not practice skills that are necessary for group projects such as patience, taking turns, and other executive functions such as organization and communication skills.

Children who experience stress and/or anxiety about interacting with other people may need professional support and may benefit from counseling or assessment from medical professionals. But most children who are gifted are able to interact great with other people when they are provided with opportunities to practice social and emotional skills.

Keep in mind that gifted traits do include characteristics that can create hardships for social situations and intensify emotional responses. Statistics show that gifted children are also often victims of bullying—more likely of the verbal type versus the physical type, but some deal with both as well. (See Gifted Children and Bullying: Victims and Perpetrators, at

http://www.education.com/reference/article/gifted-children-bullying-victims-perpetrators/.) In other words, gifted children may need support for not only their own social emotional issues but are at a high risk of becoming targets for other children who need work on their own social issues too.

Misdiagnosis

Gifted children may express themselves with behaviors that mimic other types of mental health or behavioral diagnoses. For example, the intensities related to gifted children that may make a child more likely to run around and need to wiggle during their days could be mistaken for attention deficit disorders, and their impulsivity and excitement about learning new things and asking questions could be seen as hyperactivity.

There are articles and even books available on the topic of gifted misdiagnosis and it is recommended that caretakers and other professionals become as familiar with the issues surrounding misdiagnosis as possible. It is important to also recognize that children may indeed have multiple diagnoses and giftedness can go hand in hand with learning challenges too. But medical professionals should have gifted training in order to best tell the differences between very similar behaviors. (See the SENG misdiagnosis initiative information at

http://sengifted.org/programs/misdiagnosis-initiative/.)

Twice exceptionalities

Children who are gifted and also have other learning challenges or multiple diagnoses are considered to be twice exceptional or called "2e." These children experience more frustrations than gifted children without learning challenges because they are bright enough to know what they want to communicate or do, but they are unable to do it as well as they would like. This is an area of frustration for parents, caretakers, and educators at times as well, because they can see the frustration of the child, plus they would like to be able to support the child with what they need, but the child has many levels of needs. Children who are twice exceptional often express their desire to continue to learn new and novel things, while still having accommodations for their challenges, but only if those accommodations do not limit their abilities to proceed through advanced learning or do not make them feel like other kids will think there is something wrong with them. (See, I am a Twice Exceptional Student, at

http://www.edweek.org/ew/articles/2012/03/28/26collins.h31.html.)

Twice exceptional students are entitled by federal law to special education services, but also can and should be given gifted services as well. If you suspect your young child has possible twice exceptional issues you should contact your local public school special education department and discuss options for early learning support services. The earlier you can identify their challenges, the earlier they can be supported in ways that allow them to excel later in life with support for their gifted traits too.

Gifted vs. Other Stuff

A somewhat simplified chart to give you examples of how hard it can be to tell between gifted traits and other potential diagnoses at times

Gifted	ADHD	ODD	Mood Disorders
Child may have "roller coaster emotions" and react harshly to those emotions due to thinking deeply about issues or having intense reactions	Child may seem unable to control emotional responses	Child may seem unruly or act in ways that show disrespect and dislike for authority	Child may have deep anxiety or depression or be unable to work through his/her emotional responses compared with other children
May focus intensely on things they are interested in, and ignore other things they are less interested in	Child may be unable to focus on tasks	Child may not listen or follow directions if they do not want to do so	Child may seem defiant or unable to engage with other children
Child may be impulsive and not be able to control what they say or do easily because they are excited about learning or their mind is going faster than their ability to express their thoughts	Child may be impulsive and say and do things that are bothersome or inappropriate and not think about consequences	Child will struggle to follow rules or listen to others and may cause power struggles in order to avoid dealing with certain people or situations	Child may have intense reactions to what others say and/or do, and need assistance with working through their emotional responses

Questions to ask to determine whether the issues are gifted-related or something else:

-Are you seeing these behaviors in all areas of the child's life, or just in particular situations? (For example, can the child sit still to play games, but is not sitting still during math class?)

-Are they issues that cause serious problems for the child, or are they just annoying or easily ignored? (For example, if the child is unable to function in school or is throwing serious tantrums, that would be a different issue than if the child is just making a noise or reacting in silly ways that can be easily ignored or diverted.)

-Does the child have many social-emotional characteristics that are commonly found in gifted individuals? (For example, if the child has many gifted traits it is likely the child is gifted or twice exceptional.)

**Keep in mind that many children are twice exceptional, which means they could be both gifted and have other diagnoses.

4

Identifying potential gifted traits

in infants, 0-12 months

It is much more difficult to identify gifted traits in infants who are nonverbal and who have limited motor skills, compared with school aged children. But there are clues that you may be able to identify early on in a child's life that show that the child is advanced for their age in comparison to what the "average" baby should be doing.

Children who are formally identified as gifted in their elementary years share some common traits that when we go backwards and look at the characteristics of older children as infants, to see what types of traits they had during the infant years. These traits often include advanced neurological, psychomotor, and communication responses.

A longitudinal study by Terman in 1925 where they followed 1,528 children having an IQ of 135 or above, they found retrospectively that those gifted children walked about a month earlier than other children and developed language 3.5 months earlier than other children in the study.

Other studies (such as the ones cited in the following articles: http://www.qagtc.org.au/files/Article%20for%20February%20QAGTC.pdf and http://mcgt.net/preschool-behaviors-in-gifted-children) have shown that infants who later are determined to be gifted may be more active than other babies and that they specifically, showed an ability for "calm wakefulness" for more than 8 minutes compared to the average amount of 4 to 5 minutes for other newborns. That means that those infants were able to absorb things from their environment while awake, about twice as long as other infants their same ages.

Parents of these advanced children remembered being told their babies seem "unusually alert," and they could see this alertness in particular when the infants made eye contact soon after birth and continued that interaction and awareness with the world around them. They also make eye contact while feeding, while other babies may not have that ability at such a young age.

Dr. Linda Silverman presents the following "Early Signs of Giftedness":

-Unusual alertness in infancy

-long attention span in infancy

-less need for sleep in infancy

-smiling or recognizing caretakers early

-advanced progression through developmental milestones

-high activity level

-extraordinary feats of memory

Gifted babies may have early movement skills such as sitting early, moving their head more and earlier, and grasping purposefully. This is followed by early crawling and walking too. Advances can be noticed throughout the first year of life, which then gives them more freedom of movement and they may become more autonomous earlier than other infants.

This also means that they are able to learn more about the environment around them because they can access it earlier than other babies do. It also exposes them to situations that may cause them fear or anxiety because they can push their physical limits or get themselves into situations they don't know how to get out of (pulling the tail of the family dog, pulling themselves up on things and not knowing how to get down, etc.). This is just the beginning of experiences where they will be able to access situations that they may not really be ready for, physically and/or emotionally, and this is one reason gifted children have different social-emotional responses and intensities, because of their early exposure to cognitive challenges.

This early coordination also extends to earlier hand-to-eye coordination (a rapid response to gaze and they can focus their eyes on moving objects through 90% to either side, moving both the eyes and the head). And this alertness leads them to also be more aware of their senses (auditory, visual, olfactory, etc.).

Researcher Fagan (1984) found that infants paid more attention to novel objects than those they had previously viewed. Fagan studied children at 7 months and then again at 3 years and 5 years and found that those early novelty preferences were highly related to later intelligence. (Fagan, J.F., III (1984), The relationship of novelty preferences during infancy to later intelligence and later recognition memory. Intelligence, 8(4), 339-346.)

Gifted children also begin babbling early (around 4 months old on average, with the imitation of animal noises around 22 months). Studies of gifted children's infancy show that most of the children were early talkers, and research shows that early acquisition of language skills does correlate with later intellectual success. (See Gottfried, Gifted IQ: Early Developmental Aspects, The Fullerton Longitudinal Study, Plenum Press, 1994, at

https://books.google.com/books?hl=en&lr=&id=CfHlxHn8vZcC&oi=f

nd&pg=PR3&dq=infant+gifted+research&ots=wGZ2UoCJ9w&sig=j

E0UxQv9WevDSQxgFG14fsW3pzl#v=onepage&q=infant%20gifted

%20research&f=false, page 8.)

In one study, Gross (1993) recorded linguistic precocity with the mean age at which 15 children in the study spoke their first word being 9.7 months with a standard deviation of 4.85 months. The study found that children who were gifted could "link words into meaning earlier and with greater degrees of complexity than were their age peers." (Gross, M.U.M. (1993). Exceptionally gifted children. Routledge: New York)

Gifted infants may also exhibit emotional sensitivity that can be seen from the early formation of attachments, and empathetic responses to sensing others' distress and/or anxiety. This means that they may react by crying when they hear other children or adults crying or act nervous around people who don't seem to be happy. They watch people closely and seem interested in animals and treat them gently.

Infants who are (later identified as) gifted, often like to be able to move around and have constant interaction. They do not like to be left in their infant seats and almost always want to have people in the room interacting with him or her. Some of these babies are able to entertain themselves, but others want constant interaction and expect caretakers to actually play with them, whereas other infants may be content to be alone more. Sometimes these infants sleep less than other babies, using their wakeful hours to continue to explore their environments and practice their motor skills and communication efforts. This can be exhausting to parents who are in need of sleep themselves, and who have spent the day providing their baby with constant attention. This is where support from other family members and friends is important to the well-being of the parents and the infants.

Gifted infants often have longer attention spans than other similar-aged babies. They seem intently focused on figuring things out around them and may cry when objects they are fascinated with are removed. This may be related to intrinsic motivation, which is one of the areas that has been historically linked with high intellect and achievement, as they clue in on what they are interested in and seem intent to get a hold of those objects or do not want to let them go until they are done exploring them.

It is not possible to really know exactly how an infant will grow and develop, and some infants who seem advanced may plateau or their development may even out and become more average. But when children exhibit advanced development patterns and are ready for more challenges or opportunities for exploration, we shouldn't hold them back.

By finding safe and loving ways to expand their world during those periods of interest, and by holding them close and loving them through their frustrations we can provide them with just the right mix of comfort and adventure. If they end up being formally identified as gifted later, then you and their team of support people can deal with what that means for that child at that time. And if they don't end up being formally identified later, that is ok too—it just means their support will have to come from their other team members, such as parents, physicians, counselors and all of the other people who step in and continue to support them as they grow up. In the meanwhile, there is no harm in treating smart babies like the brilliant and amazing beings they are!

Development milestones		
	Normal Development	30% Advanced
Gross motor		
Rolls over	3 months	2.1 months
Sits alone	7	4.9
Stands alone well	11	7.7
Walks alone	12.5	8.8
Fine motor		
Plays with rattle	3	2.1
Holds object between finger and thumb	9	6.3
Scribbles spontaneously	13	9.1
Language development		
Vocalizes two different sounds	2.3	1.6
Says first word	7.9	5.5
Responds to name	9	6.3
Babbles with intonation	12	8.4
Vocabulary of 4-6 words	15	10.5

Information from Davidson Gifted, in an article by David Farmer (1996), from Harrison (1995) pp 24 & 33, with Harrison attributing her information to Hall, EG & Skinner, N (1980) Somewhere to turn: strategies for parents of the gifted and talented children. New York: Teachers College Press. See http://www.davidsongifted.org/Search-Database/entry/A10106.

Signs this 0-12 month-old may be gifted:

SIGN	Yes	No
Calm wakefulness of around 8 minutes (versus 4-5 minutes for other infants)		
Moves head and focusing on objects through 90% on each side		
Grasps items purposefully at an early age		
Cries when objects are removed from their hands earlier than other infants pay attention to things in their hands		
Babbling by around 4 months		
First word spoken at about 9.7 months		
Sits early compared with other infants their age		
More aware of lights, smells, sounds than other infants their age		
Need for constant interaction and novelty at a young age and continuing		

5

Supporting potential giftedness

in infants, 0-12 months

"How might the promotion of giftedness be different than it was 10 years ago, or 50 years ago, especially given the fact that we now know that infants are incredibly more responsive than we had assumed?"

— Patricia Haensly, Ph.D., *Parenting the Gifted*, Gifted Child Today, 2004

Formal gifted services often start after kindergarten when K-12 education begins. However, there is nothing stopping preschool caretakers/educators and parents from supporting potentially gifted babies in the meantime. In fact, it may help these infants interact with the world in ways that support their needs and increase their developmental skills.

There are some researchers who believe giftedness can be predicted in infancy, but this is rare. Researcher Goswami (1992) found that the ability to recognize relational or structural similarity, the basis of analogical reasoning, is present from the first months of life. And there are some experts who have come up with methods for assessing the analogical thinking of even very young children, including infants and toddlers (DeLoache, Simcock, & Marzolf, 2004; Goswami, 1992; Holyoak & Thasgard, 1997; Schafer, 2005). Yet, the reliability of those measures is controversial, with many gifted education experts believing that actual intellect cannot be reliably measured until children are school-aged or older.

Regardless of whether you believe you can obtain reliable formal identification for giftedness at such a young age, it is important that as parents record their observations when they start noticing that an infant is doing advanced things, such as being especially alert, or mimicking language, or showing advanced motor skills.

Research on gifted infancy has relied quite heavily on records that were kept in baby books, as oral recollection is less reliable than actual records that were written down. It may seem as though baby book entries are more useful as family remembrances for parents to review with their child when they are older and "ooh and ahhh" over the cute photos and things like pieces of baby hair from their first haircuts. But the records parents keep regarding developmental progress could someday help them show advanced abilities that may help with their intellectual evaluations. This is not necessarily something that school officials will ask for, but it definitely is worth keeping in mind in case it does help to show your child's actual skill levels from a young age. Therefore, try to keep records on their skills and characteristics, especially as you notice advanced behaviors.

According to an article by David Farmer (1996), "Perhaps the most useful first piece of advice is to keep good, dated records of your child's development, not just of sitting and walking, but of the less glamorous stages too, such as grasping an object with finger and thumb, first using a two-word sentence, and first turning of the pages of a book etc." (http://www.davidsongifted.org/Search-Database/entry/A10106).

Parents should start building a team of professionals and other support people who can help them with identifying and supporting their child's gifted traits. This should include talking with their children's pediatricians to begin the discussion about potential giftedness. This can help them to prevent potential misdiagnosis issues or misunderstandings between team members and can help identify any possible twice exceptional issues.

Other team members could include friends, family members who are directly or indirectly involved with raising the child (this includes long-distance contacts who can be sources of support when parenting is harder!) and also, consider finding educators in the community (either formal preschool teachers and administrators, or even home care providers or those who offer occasional workshops,) so you can start planning for educational experiences and at least be able to have another opinion regarding the child's progress and what is considered "age appropriate." It is often nice to collaborate with others who can help provide you with ideas for community events and interactions that will allow your bright infant to be exposed to new concepts and experiences.

Parents of smart babies should always find ways to provide their little ones with stimulating and caring environments. There should always be a safety net of loving arms to retreat to when they explore farther than their comfort area. But those arms should be careful not to limit the child's progress as they grow and become more confident with their skills.

Infants need a lot of time to sleep and eat, but they also spend their waking hours absorbing information from their environment around them. Provide them with interesting things to look at with contrasting colors (babies love black and white designs when they are younger, and then prefer bright primary colors.) Fill their world around them with pre-reading materials such as photos of interesting scenes and letters and numbers. Read to them often and let them hold and even chew on baby books when they are able to hold things on their own. The more familiar with books they are, the more likely they will feel comfortable exploring them as readers.

Take walks and talk with them about what they see. Repeat words to them so they start thinking more about the sounds and how words work together. The more they feel like their parents are interested in what they are doing and the more they hear words, the more likely they will be to expand their vocabulary and connect the words with more and more advanced concepts.

Research has shown that early language is a type of music to infants' ears. According to an article by Brandt, Gebrian and Slevc in Frontiers in Auditory Cognitive Neuroscience, a specialty of Frontiers in Psychology:

> Language is a compromise between what adults need to say and children's ability to process and perform what they hear. And, crucially, what infants hear is, by the broad definition above, a form of music…. We argue not that language has a privileged status in the newborn brain, but rather that *music* has a privileged status that enables us to acquire not only

the musical conventions of our native culture, but also enables us to learn our native language. *Without the ability to hear musically, we would be unable to learn language.* (Brandt et al., 2012)

Therefore, it is important that infants be exposed to music and that they hear a lot of sing-song words. This is supported further by Brandt, Gebrian and Slevc, as they state, "The aspects of language that differ the most from music come later: *the further removed a feature of language is from music, the later it is learned.*" (https://www.ncbi.nlm.nih.gov/pmc/articles/PMC3439120/)

The more infants are exposed to new and novel things and are encouraged to explore and play, the more likely they are to grow and flourish even when things get frustrating at times. Parenting babies that don't like to sleep, need constant attention, do best with lots of talking and singing, and throw fits when they are feeling a mismatch between their cognitive abilities and what their little bodies do, are definitely a lot of work. But when things are going well for them and they give you one of their big hugs or brilliant grins then it all seems worth it!

Gifted Infant Issues and Questions

Record your questions or notes here:

6

Identifying potential gifted traits in toddlers, 12-30 months

Gifted researcher, Terman, did research on gifted children way back in 1925, and he found that toddlers who were gifted often showed advanced psychomotor development, including walking one month earlier than the average, and acquiring language three and a half months earlier than average, with the early acquisition of reading as well.

Other research has shown that their language development is very important in influencing other social-emotional development. Lists have been created by researchers who have explored the histories of children who are formally identified later in life and many of the traits stem from the young child being able to use communication skills to interact with the world around them. (See Dr. Deborah L. Ruf's article, Preschool Behaviors in Gifted Children, 2009, at http://mcgt.net/preschool-behaviors-in-gifted-children.)

Their advanced language skills include advanced subskill areas, including the following: advanced vocabulary for their age, using language in original and meaningful ways, a richness of expression, elaboration, and fluency (Cukiercorn et al., 2008, http://www.southernearlychildhood.org/upload/pdf/Recognizing_Gift edness_Defining_High_Ability_in_Young_Children_Jesse_R_Cukie rkorn_Frances_A_Karnes_Sandra_J_Manning_Heather_Houston_ Kevin_Besnoy_Vol_36_No_2.pdf). Their advanced speaking skills also are connected with advanced memory skills, too (Lewis, Feiring, & McGuffog, 1986; Lewis & Michalson, 1985). Which means that children who start out with advanced language skills have a distinct advantage for processing information that they can remember at an earlier age than like-aged peers. Cukiercorn et al. (2008) states that these linguistically skilled toddlers can therefore "express their ideas, seek information through questioning, and interact verbally with their parents and other family members at an age when other children are only beginning to experiment with oral communication."

And all of those skills impact the child's development of social-emotional skills, as they are able to express themselves and interact more with others, which can mean positive things, such as them being able to express their desires and needs. But it also can mean more challenges, because often their like-age peers are not able to communicate with them as well as they may be able to speak, which can be frustrating for gifted toddlers who don't understand why their playmates don't speak with them as much. And it also may set them up for standoffs with authority figures, as they can communicate their wishes and those wishes may not always be what they get. So, the "terrible twos" can be even more challenging with gifted children who not only refuse to back down when their hearts are set on getting their way, but they are also often know what to say to really push your buttons. (Plus, remember that with their advanced development, they may hit those "terrible twos" before they even have their second birthday!)

Similarly, gifted toddlers often are very motivated to be competent in the things they try to do. Their little bodies do not always comply and sometimes those desires are quickly stopped by the adults around them for safety reasons (it's not safe to run out in the road or to try to swim in that pool by themselves, so caretakers have to set limits sometimes), and gifted toddlers are quick to throw tantrums when they don't get to continue with their plans to explore the world.

During the 1- to 2-year-old ages, gifted toddlers have an obvious interest in competence and they throw fits when not permitted to do things themselves. They are tenacious and think they need to do things in their own way and that they are not done until they decide they are. They are not easily distracted from what they want to do and they don't easily fall for tricks to avert their attention from their goals. They have long attention spans and have a strong interest in letters, numbers, books, and talking and they know many letters, numbers and colors. They can more clearly understand the speech of adults and they talk a lot. They often know how to count and organize and know many colors and shades. Many know the alphabet in order or isolation.

They have surprisingly good eye-hand coordination and enjoy toys like shape sorters, puzzles and often want to play with toys that are beyond their stated age level, including machinery, computers, and implements that are complex and maybe delicate. That being said, they do not usually destroy those delicate items on purpose or chew on books like other children of the same age might do (they likely have learned that books are full of stories and colorful pictures if they have had previous experience with them).

Emotionally, gifted toddlers have a lot of empathy and they try hard to please. This can mean their feelings are easily hurt. They notice aesthetic things like beauty in nature and pay attention to the feelings of others. Although they ask "why" a lot and insist on answers to it. They clearly exhibit a sense of humor and can be a lot of fun to laugh with. They enjoy puns and can use language in creative ways to be funny.

Music remains important to them and they enjoy singing songs. They often know the words and melody of songs they hear a lot and can sing along. They enjoy the arts and can draw pictures and tell you stories about what they've drawn. They like to build and can stack towers of 6 blocks or more.

Gifted one and two-year-olds can sometimes seem bossy. They like to tell other children what to do and if they do not comply they may lose interest in them. Others may think that your child seems "spoiled" at times because they see them expect to get their way (and may see them get what they asked for often). But a lot of the time it is easier to give in to their requests (which may be reasonable and well thought-through compared to the requests of other kids their age that may be more impulsive), than to argue with them.

Dr. Inderbir Kaur Sandhu compiled some of the advanced milestones of gifted children in the one to two-year-old ages (found at http://www.brainy-child.com/expert/early-signs-giftedness.shtml, ND):

- Ability to form two word phrases by 14 months
- Ability to understand instructions by 18 months
- Ability to say and understand many words before 18 months

- Could stay still and enjoy a TV programs (e.g., Sesame Street) by the age of 1

- Has favorite TV shows/VCD/DVDs by age 1

- Appears to require less sleep (yet not sleepy or irritable due to lack of sleep)

- Recognition of letters/alphabets by age 2

- Recognition and rote counting of numbers 1 – 10 or higher by age 2

- Recognition of colors by age 2

- Recognition of first word by age 2

- Interest in puzzles by age 2

- Has long attention span in interest areas by age 2

- Ability to form at least 3-word sentence by age 2

- Interest in time by age 2

Researcher Laurence Vaivre-Douret, 2011 (in Developmental and Cognitive Characteristics of "High-Level Potentialities" (Highly Gifted) Children, as found at https://www.hindawi.com/journals/ijpedi/2011/420297/#B57) lists the following advanced characteristics of the toddler years:

Language Skills:

- Making their first "sentence" (the association of two words), around 18 months.

- Their mastery of language shows up in their fluent use of words that are appropriate and therefore deliberate, (appropriate usage of adverbs, verb tenses, and so forth).

- Curious about their environment, for instance seeking to identify letters at an early age or recognizing the written letters on posters and in newspapers.

- An early interest in the meanings of words and in reproducing letters, so that around 34 months there are the beginnings of a form of spontaneous "writing" although the letters are not yet known.

Cognitive functioning:

- Excellent information-processing abilities may be noted (detection, perceptive discrimination, storage, and recall).

- Advanced working memory, immediate memory being prominent in their daily functioning, for instance in what they observe (makes of cars, etc.).

- They can appear very early on as being "into everything," eager, and curious, for instance, taking every object apart and exhausting their parents.

- They prefer complex games, and later on, intellectual challenges.

- They are always ready to experiment and innovate, they have creative skills, in particular in construction games, and, as early as two years of age, they take an interest in life and earth sciences, astronomy, metaphysics (life and death), and in books.

Here is a chart showing more of the milestones that gifted toddlers may hit early.

Development milestones	.	.
	Normal Development	30% Advanced
Vocabulary of 20 words	21	14.7
Combines several words spontaneously	21	14.7
Uses simple sentences	24	16.8
Uses personal pronouns	24	16.8
Walks up stairs	18	12.6
Turns pages of book	18	12.6
Runs well	24	16.8
Jumps with both feet	30	21
Rides tricycle using pedals	36	25.2

From information at http://www.davidsongifted.org/Search-Database/entry/A10106

Signs this 12-30 month-old may be gifted:

SIGN	Yes	No
walks one month earlier than the average		
acquires language three and a half months earlier than average, with two-word sentences by 14 months and		
Has advanced vocabulary for their age, using language in original and meaningful ways, a richness of expression, elaboration, and fluency		
Is able to process information that they can remember at an earlier age than like-aged peers		
Expresses their desires and needs and have more intense fits when they are not given what they want		
Shows frustration with other toddlers who are less verbal or have lower vocabulary skills		
Has long attention spans and have a strong interest in letters, numbers, books, and talking and they know many letters, numbers and colors		

Is able to think of things they want to do, but shows frustration when their little bodies physically can't do the things they want them to		
Requires less sleep and does not seem affected by less sleep		

7

Supporting potential giftedness in toddlers, 12-30 months

Some of the gifted characteristics that appear during the toddler years can be seen as problematic, such as exploration that causes the child to be in potential danger, and asking the question "why" several times a day and throwing fits when they don't get their way. Therefore, it is important that potentially gifted traits are identified and supported, but equally important that parents and caretakers have a support system too. Parents and caretakers should continue to talk with the team they have hopefully put together by now (including other parents/friends/relatives, teachers, caretakers, counselors, pediatricians, etc.) about any possible issues.

Social-emotional support

During these years, it is critical to not only support the child with novel and interesting things to think about, but also to start thinking about ways to provide more social-emotional support. When gifted toddlers are pushing their caretaker's buttons, they often are having frustration moments of their own. Find ways to reassure them of your interest and support and talk about your feelings so that they understand why their behaviors are problematic at times.

Allow them to explore things without pushing them. Parents of gifted children get a bad reputation when other people don't understand gifted characteristics or needs and they think that when a child is doing advanced things, that the parents must be pushing them. This is often not the case, as gifted children are intrinsically motivated and often push the parents more than the parents push them to grow and learn. That being said, don't let them exhaust themselves with learning opportunities (such as trying to sit too long to try to read a book if they are getting antsy), because they need to still be children and play as much as possible at this age.

Asynchrony

A related issue is to always keep in mind the concept of asynchrony, as gifted children will appear to act older than they really are at times (talking about deep concepts or showing you something they have learned,) and then they may act even younger about something else (for example, not sharing a toy with a sibling or curling up on the couch and crying like there is no tomorrow because they don't want their sandwich cut a certain way). They are still little kids and even at their best, they still need all the same love and support that other toddlers need (and sometimes more, because their intense emotional responses may make them have extra anxiety, fear, sadness, etc.).

Play

Pretend play is a huge part of the development of cognitive skills in toddler aged children. Morelock, Brown, and Morrissey (2003) found that the toddlers they studied made huge cognitive gains when their mothers did pretend play with them and the mothers talked with the toddler using analogies and mentioned links to real life, involving connections between the toddlers' past and current experiences and knowledge. (Morelock, M. J., Brown, P. M., &

Morrissey, A. M. (2003). Pretend play and maternal scaffolding: Comparisons of toddlers with advanced development, typical development, and hearing impairment. Roeper Review, 26, 41-51.) Those mothers who had a higher use of real-world links with their 2-year-olds were linked to more extensive pretend play and advanced deductive reasoning in their children. (Mills, M., & Funnell, E. (1983). Experience and cognitive processing. In S. Meadows (Ed.), Developing thinking (pp. 161-187). London, UK: Methuen.) According to Morelock, M. J., Brown, P. M., & Morrissey, A. M. (2003), those findings suggest that "by introducing verbal elements of abstraction, complexity, and challenge into their play interactions, the mothers of the high IQ children were providing a qualitatively different play experience for their children from an early age."

Fowler (1981) also found that intensive caregiver stimulation from an early age plays a significant role in the development of giftedness. (Fowler, W. (1981). Case studies of cognitive precocity: The role of exogenous and endogenous stimulation in early mental development. Journal of Applied Developmental Psychology, 2, 319-367.)

It is important for parents to provide opportunities for pretend play and to ask their toddlers questions about what they are doing and allow the toddlers to participate in the imaginary story development too. The more the child is able to interact during the play, the more they work on their vocabulary and process new concepts and ideas. Not to mention, it is more fun for everyone when those little personalities start to show and the imaginary adventures get even more entertaining!

Reading

Continue to read with your toddler and allow him/her to pick out books they enjoy reading. Libraries are wonderful places for new and novel books and provide opportunities for toddlers to interact with other toddlers during free activity times. There are a lot of things you can do at the library with children in this age group, for example:

"More and more libraries are instituting programs designed for toddlers 18 to 36 months old… parents and children participate in activities that may include reading aloud, storytelling, fingerplays, rhymes, and songs. Because this age is a crucial time in the development of language skills, the value of these events lies in giving parents or caregivers the background on how to stimulate and encourage a child's development as well as entertaining the toddlers." (Kathryn Perkinson (1996), Helping Your Child Use the Library, http://files.eric.ed.gov/fulltext/ED400833.pdf)

You can use reading time to hold your child close or sit with them on the floor so they also benefit from having contact with you and so that reading is thought of as a safe and fun activity. This also promotes cuddling during a time when gifted children still need to feel embraced by their parents, but they are always on the go and sometimes don't sit still long enough for cuddle time!

8

Identifying potential gifted traits in early learners, 30-48 months

Gifted children between the age of two and a half years old and four years old are in a stage when parents and other people are more likely to start noticing how advanced they are. They walk and talk well, they hold conversations about things that interest them, and they enjoy joking and laughing. They can be more easily compared with other children because they are more verbal now and their peers also are, and they likely take part in social events such as play groups, preschool, and activities at local parks where they are with other children. In fact, according to Dr. Linda

Silverman (ND, http://australiangiftedsupport.com/ccmword/wp-content/uploads/2014/12/1352283166.pdf):

> In one study, 35% of the parents recognized their child's giftedness between ages 3 and 5. The other 65% were either informed or recognized their child's giftedness after age six."

This means that during these ages, advanced behaviors and skills stand out even more than in the past.

These gifted "early learners" like to talk and ask a lot of questions. They now are asking more than just "why?" and expect you to give them answers to complicated questions. They really enjoy debating and practicing their arguing skills.

Part of their questions have to do with their increased worrying at this stage. They think about the world around them a lot more than before, and they want to make sense of things that often don't even make sense to adults. They care about justice and fairness and they want to know the how and why of advanced things. Not only do they ask the questions, but they want to actually understand the answers so they listen closely, unlike most similar-aged peers.

They like to play games with rules and enjoy making new rules and discussing strategies. They don't understand when other nongifted agemates or even adults do not understand what they are trying to explain and they can be very bossy because they want people to follow their ideas.

Gifted children at this age are also practicing their negotiation skills. They may practice their charm, with blinking eyes and big smiles, and then when that doesn't work they may cry and try that tactic. If you give in to their tactics they will use that strategy again and maybe cry longer or increase their charms. They are cleverly manipulative at this age.

With all of those questions, parents may get tired of having to be encyclopedias, so luckily kids this age also enjoy looking at information in books. This is a great age to become members of the local library if you haven't already. And since gifted children at this age also enjoy working on computers, doing online searches can be fun too.

These advanced early learners are often very creative and enjoy doing arts and crafts. But they may throw fits when they can't replicate the ideas in their minds and perfectionism may rear its frustrating head.

Dr. Linda Silverman lists these traits as early signs of giftedness in this age group:

- Intense interest in books

- Keen powers of observation

- Ability to generalize concepts

- Recognition of letters before age 2

- Ability to put together a 20-piece puzzle before age 3

- Asks complex, probing questions

- Early interest in time—clocks, calendars

- Imaginary playmates

http://australiangiftedsupport.com/ccmword/wp-content/uploads/2014/12/1352283166.pdf

According to Abroms & Gollin (1980), by age 3, gifted children can better understand the thoughts, emotions, and viewpoints of others. They found that gifted early learners at this age may exhibit these traits related to these types of social cognition:

- generosity

- sharing of possessions

- sympathy for others

- the desire to attend to other's needs at an early age.

However, Dr. Deborah Lovecky (2004) found that peer relationships between gifted youngsters and other children their age were difficult, due to them not having much in common to talk about, so gifted young children often made up solitary fantasy play situations. They also liked playing with older children, but the older children did not enjoy playing with such younger kids, so many gifted early learners in this age group struggled to have reciprocal friendships and instead settled for independent play or they made up cooperative games and the other children followed along based on the strength of the gifted child's imaginations. (Different Minds: Gifted Children with AD/HD, Asperger Syndrome, and Other Learning Deficits,

https://books.google.com/books?id=tycQBQAAQBAJ&pg=PA317&l
pg=PA317&dq=Abroms+%26+Gollin+(1980),&source=bl&ots=1wX
uzfpodo&sig=Wh4CqkiMICE9TCJGKrj_6nRNQDU&hl=en&sa=X&v
ed=0ahUKEwi_4p60i5PRAhUKQiYKHZXWAaoQ6AEIGjAA#v=one
page&q=Abroms%20%26%20Gollin%20(1980)%2C&f=false)

Many non-gifted children in this age range tend to play next to each other, but not coordinate their made-up stories. However, rather than just using parallel play, young children in the 2 to 3-year-old age range who are gifted tend to initiate their play sessions with other children and they enjoy playing more cooperatively than their nongifted peers (Barnett, & Fiscella, 1985; Lupkowski, 1989). These early learners who are gifted may use a complex type of management of other children they are playing with, directing them away from "egocentric thought, toward decentralized thought, which is a trait more typical of 6- and 7-year-olds" (Wright, 1990).

Since gifted early learners have advanced language abilities, they are able to easily explain what they are thinking and often can be seen as being "bossy." Other children may gravitate to their intensity and abilities to orchestrate play in dramatic ways, so they may be attractive play partners. However, they also may have intense emotional reactions when others do not follow their directions, which may lead to social issues with their peers.

Dr. Inderbir Kaur Sandhu (http://www.brainy-child.com/expert/early-signs-giftedness.shtml, ND) explains even more characteristics of giftedness in this age range:

- Early and extensive language development and vocabulary, forms grammatically correct sentences as compared to peers
- Interest in computers (not video games)
- Ability to solve a 20-piece puzzle by age 3
- Has a vivid imagination (includes having imaginary friends)
- Extraordinary feats of memory
- Extreme curiosity and asks many questions
- Specific talent (if any), such as artistic ability or an unusual facility for numbers—becomes more apparent by age 4
- Ability to memorize and recall facts easily
- Early development of a sense of humor

- Ability to do one-to-one counting for small quantities by age 3

- Recognition of simple signs and own written name by age 3

- Ability to write letters, numbers, words, and their names between 3 and 4 years

- Ability to read easy readers by age 4

- Rather independent on the computer by age 4

- Demonstration of musical aptitude just after 2

- Ability to do simple addition and subtraction by age 4

- High degrees of mathematical understanding by age 4

Development milestones	Normal Development	30% Advanced
Jumps with both feet	30	21
Rides tricycle using pedals	36	25.2
Throws ball	48	33.6
Skips with alternate feet	60	42
Draws person with two body parts	48	33.6
Draws recognizable person with body	60	42

From information at http://www.davidsongifted.org/Search-Database/entry/A10106

Signs this 30-48 month-old may be gifted:

SIGN	Yes	No
Asks a lot of "why" questions and wants to know a lot about everything		
Enjoys playing games and making up rules earlier than like-age peers, and can get frustrated when others don't agree with their interpretations of the rules		
Can be cleverly manipulative compared with their like-age peers		
Has perfectionism issues and throws fits when they can't do something "just right"		
Is interested in putting together puzzles and can do 20-piece puzzles by age 3		
Interested in time (clocks, calendars, planning events)		
Enjoys playing with older peers		
By age 2 or 3 they are interested in doing more cooperative play than their peers, who often are still doing parallel play at those ages		
Can count one-to-one quantities by age 3		
Can read easy readers by age 4		
Can skip, jump, ride bikes, etc. earlier than their peers		

9

Supporting potential giftedness in early learners, 30-48 months

It is important to realize that the needs of the gifted early learner during the ages of two and a half through three years may not all be ones of simply finding the right materials or enrichment activities. Social emotional interactions are at the forefront of development during this time.

These children are still asking a lot of questions and their vocabulary is advanced enough that their questions may be much deeper and the child may be much more invested in your answers than they have been in the past. They care a lot about serious issues and can dwell on things that are scary or that cause them stress, such as things they see on televisions (crimes, natural disasters, etc.) or things they hear (parent arguments, songs on the radio that discuss violence, and more). This is an age of worrying, and some big phobias may surface at this time, as well as obsessions with solving the problems of the world or preparing for surviving natural disasters.

But these worries and fears may cause the gifted early learner to have intense emotional reactions and behaviors that may seem unrelated but are stress-releasing activities when the child feels overwhelmed with emotions.

The interactions between gifted children and caretakers can be demanding. Children at this age have a need for independence and leadership that caretakers may not be ready for. There also may be power-struggles regarding things that the child wants to do (similar to struggles the child has had during younger years, because asynchrony is still at play and they may act much younger at times).

Gifted children at this age may be more sensitive to environmental things than other children their age. For example, they may be embarrassed to use a shared bathroom because they want more privacy. They may have trouble taking naps because they are so excited about learning, or they may have sporadic napping patterns that may cause power struggles if caretakers have to stick to a schedule. They may hear caretakers discussing them and may be sensitive to what is said. They are more aware of wanting to please people and may have perfectionism traits too. It is important to be aware of their frustrations and to talk with them about their concerns. This is a good time to really invest in mutual respect, as their self-esteem is building now and they are sponges for good role modeling (or the opposite), now.

Preschool readiness

At this age, a child is likely ready for some type of formalized education program. This is not necessary if parents or caretakers provide the child with learning experiences at home or in a home daycare. But research shows that preschool programs help young learners to be more prepared for kindergarten. Many states offer free or reduced preschool courses for children when they are four years old, however those programs should be evaluated for effectiveness for an advanced learner and preparedness for working with a child with gifted traits.

If you do decide to enroll your gifted child in a preschool program, it is helpful to prepare him or her for the expectations of an educational environment. Researchers suggest teaching the child skills such as social-behavioral goals and functional skills that will be required in the preschool program, prior to the child actually enrolling. You can talk with your child about the program's schedule and how it will work for them (including talking about any food services they will have or how they will take their snacks or lunches with them, and how potty-training or bathroom activities will work). They should be encouraged to ask questions when they need to, or to reach out for help when appropriate. And discussing social skills and required classroom behaviors will be helpful, such as raising their hand during group lessons and taking turns with peers, etc. This will prepare them for success in the program and give you a chance to discuss social skills that they are working on during these ages.

Music

Musical skill continues to be as important as it was when the child was an infant and was first experiencing the sounds of language. Now the task for the young child is to gain competence with the syntax of the language, which also happens as they learn more about the culture's music. Between the ages of 2–3 years, children acquire that competence with language (e.g., Höhle et al., 2001) and with the syntax of the culture's music (Corrigall and Trainor, 2009). Continue to play music and sing with your child throughout their early childhood so as to help them develop these skills that research shows will impact their cognitive functions into their school years. Encouraging your child to sing may also impact their abilities to master their native language, but also will assist them later while understanding and learning second language sound structures (Slevc and Miyake, 2006; Lee and Hung, 2008; Delogu et al., 2010).

Extra-curricular activities

Some preschools and homeschool co-ops have preschool arts and crafts or other creative activities offered outside of the regular class times. This is a good age for gifted early learners to have access to as many new experiences as possible. If your community does not provide these types of classes, or they are expensive there are other ways you can access novel and educational experiences by taking your preschooler to local zoos, science museums, and even local parks. Bring a magnifying glass or containers to collect interesting objects like leaves and rocks to investigate further. Some regions have social media pages highlighting fun scavenger hunts such as looking for painted rocks in the local area—Perhaps your early learner would like to paint one to contribute!

Educational digital programing

The jury is out about whether television and computer screen time are helpful or harmful to young learners. However, our world is more digital than ever and future careers and educational experiences are bound to include a variety of computerized activities. This is an age where children can access stimulating activities in computerized games, videos and more. Take time to explore the internet together, including finding videos and interesting stories to discuss. Just be aware of the dangers of children on the internet and discuss safety with your children. It's never to early to put safety checks in place and make sure they are

aware of your rules.

Gifted Early Learner Issues and Questions

Record your questions or notes here:

10

Identifying potential gifted traits in preschoolers, 48-60 months

Preschool aged (four and five-year-old) children who are gifted are focused on cognitive skill building and achievement at this age. Kitano (1985) found that preschool children not only showed high levels of knowledge and cognitive abilities, but they also showed "prelogical thinking, discomfort with ambiguity, creativity, and spontaneous incorporation of academic activities into free play."

All of this thinking, combined with active imaginations, mean that gifted preschool children continue to worry about the world around them and want to talk about it. Cukierkorn et al. (2008) noted that

"Perhaps as a reflection of the gifted child's greater language fluency, preschoolers who are gifted also talk about problems, rules, and goals to a greater extent than do their average ability peers."

Gifted preschoolers are more likely to want to solve challenges and problems themselves with less help from adults than other children their age. Cukierkorn et al. (2008) gave this example of this scenario from a study by Kanevsky's (1992):

> Four and five-year-old children were given puzzles to solve in the presence of a supportive tutor who was available both to answer questions and to offer help. The young children who were intellectually gifted were more able to evaluate their own need for assistance. They asked for help and denied assistance when they felt that they could solve a step in the puzzle on their own, whereas the average four and five-year-olds seldom denied help and generally accepted the tutor's offer to help."
>
> http://www.southernearlychildhood.org/upload/pdf/Recognizing_Giftedness_Defining_High_Ability_in_Young_Children_J

Gifted children at this age may become veracious and precocious readers, excelling in text-reading speed (both oral and silent), and they may use phonetic analysis to identify nonsense words and the spelling of dictated words (Burns, Collins, & Paulsell, 1991; Jackson, 1992). This ability to read quickly and use advanced phonetic skills helps them understand what they read better. Instead of being bogged down by difficult words, they use context clues and keep forging forward. This increases their ability to absorb the story and enjoy the contents, (Jackson, 1992). Many begin reading simple books and then may read chapter books before they are five.

They have high level vocabularies and can easily memorize facts and other information. If you forget little details in conversation, they are quick to help you. They have advanced senses of humor, due to their advanced communication skills and quick wit, which may endear them to others, or may cause issues when other peers do not understand their humor, or when adults do not find it appropriate. They enjoy riddles and analogies.

They also are quite literal and may argue with you if you round numbers or talk in generalities. They have a lot of questions and a fascination about big topics like life and death. They may question the meaning of life, their own worth, and other deep issues that will need parental support. They now have abstract reasoning ability and they love theorizing. As Dr. Deborah Ruf (2009) phrases it, they are now "philosophical and speculative" (http://mcgt.net/preschool-behaviors-in-gifted-children). They may also seem to tune you out when they are involved in something they want to concentrate on, which is a skill they learn (sometimes this is mistaken for sensory issues, so keep this in mind).

Gifted preschoolers continue to be asynchronous and their bodies are still growing so they may still be frustrated at times when their bodies are not as able to do the things they want to do. That being said, this is an age when their bodies need to move. Ruf (2009) reminds us that too much focus on academics (at the cost of play), at this age can impact their abilities to fine-tune their motor skills. In other words, they still need to run around and play and explore using their bodies at this age!

These little beings continue to need to rest in between play, but even during sleep their bodies are busy—research has shown that gifted preschoolers have a greater duration of rapid eye movement (REM) sleep than other children and higher frequency of eye movement during REM sleep.

Ruff (2009) also notes that gifted children this age have a high level of emotional sensitivity which allows for the early development of values, empathy, and responsibility. They have a strong concern for others and their feelings and tend to display good self-concepts and social-emotional adjustment. They can use self-reflection but they experience intra and interpersonal conflict due to being sensitive and may struggle with feelings of being different, a need for recognition, and impatience with others.

Preschoolers who are gifted are highly curious and may be impulsive when getting excited about concepts, which may lead to a lot of "why?" questions and possible outbursts at inappropriate times. They like to learn and integrate large amounts of knowledge and their quest for novel information may seem insatiable at times, which may wear others out who are done thinking about concepts that the gifted child continues to think about and discuss.

Signs this 48-60 month-old may be gifted:

SIGN	Yes	No
Cares deeply about world issues that may seem more appropriate for older children to think about		
Exhibits moments where they are stubbornly independent		
Is very literal and will argue with you when you try to round numbers or talk in generalities		
Is voraciously interested in reading and learning about new things		
Can be deeply introspective and philosophical		
Feels different than other like-age peers and struggles with their deep empathy that can cause emotional stress at times		

May wear other people out because they don't tire of subjects as quickly as others their age do		
Is reading chapter books by age 5		
Has high vocabulary skills		

Gifted Preschooler Issues and Questions

Record your questions or notes here:

11

Supporting potential giftedness in preschoolers, 48-60 months

Gifted children who are four and five years of age are at the ages where they absorb information like sponges. It is a time where parents need to become the facilitators of educational experiences, while still supporting the gifted child's social-emotional needs for security and understanding during the times when things are more frustrating.

What to look for in preschool or other formal learning situations

Preschool children are ready for more formal learning experiences that could include preschool classes or even just group workshops. If caretakers do decide to enroll preschool aged gifted children in these types of programs, it is important to look for options that include the following things:

- Flexible groupings: meaning that children of different ages or abilities are invited to attend and those children can move between groups as needed, either by their own choice, or by careful observation by the teacher or other adults. For example, multi-aged preschool classrooms work well for gifted children whose skills may be high in some areas, yet need support in other areas. If classrooms are set by ages, on the other hand, gifted children may need to be able to move between rooms or be given differentiation in the groups that they are placed in, so as to continue to meet their need for challenge and to support their social-emotional needs too.

- Flexible resources: meaning that gifted children may need higher level materials in order to be successful, or they may need to be able to move quickly through materials and use more hands-on approaches to their learning. If a child is ready for different materials, they should not be withheld from them just due to their age. If they have learning gaps, they may need to access remedial materials in novel ways, so that they can continue to learn, without missing key concepts. This requires teachers or caretakers to find resources that allow for multiple uses or expanded play or exploration to look at more than just the initial concept. For example, hands on math manipulatives may allow for counting, sorting, or even adding, subtracting and multiplication skill building, so materials that can be used in many ways work well with gifted children who need diverse and differentiated learning options.

- Early admission or transfers: sometimes gifted young children are ready for higher level activities, so programs that allow them to enter when they are ready for the skills in the class are really helpful. If they are in a class and they need more support or need a higher level of learning, being able to transfer to another class makes it much less stressful for the teacher, the parents, and the child.

- Talking with them about issues: If educators or caretakers who are providing the learning experience are able to talk with the child about their needs and expectations, or to explain why the class is structured the way it is (or why they are using specific materials or approaches), then the gifted young child will feel more ownership of the class and be more willing to work within those specifications. Having an openness for communication between teacher, parents and children makes learning experiences more of a team effort, and everyone benefits.

- Real world applications and examples: the more that learning can be connected to real life, the more likely gifted children are to stay interested in the process and excited about the products. Finding community service opportunities and ways to bring in experts from the community can make learning opportunities even more fun and engaging.

- Novelty: any learning experience for gifted children should be novel and utilize interesting information and creative approaches so as to keep the children excited about the learning and continuously wanting to know more and learn more skills.

- Social emotional support: all learning experiences for gifted young learners should be immersed with social-emotional support and practice with social skill building. When there are situations that seem like they could be frustrating or produce anxiety in gifted learners, the teachers or facilitators should be ready to work through those concerns and keep the learning environment positive so that they children feel comfortable working on the hard parts.

- Specific praise: research shows that gifted children who are praised with generic statements, such as "you are so smart," do not develop the skills needed to persevere when the going is tough. By telling young gifted children what they did that helped them achieve success, with specific statements, such as "I like the way you worked hard and put so many different colors on that drawing of the universe," help them understand what they are doing well, and emphasizes the executive functions and social-emotional traits that help them succeed long-term.

Spirituality and gifted children

Preschool children are more curious about big issues such as life and death and they are often very philosophical. This leads to discussions that parents can support and explain the family's beliefs regarding ethics, religion, and more.

Piechowski (2001) discusses many instances of gifted young children discussing topics related to religious or spiritual thoughts and recollections, pointing to the fact that young childhood is a time when children are ready for, and perhaps craving, more information about issues that we may not always have exact answers for. This is a time when religion may become more interesting to gifted youngsters, and if their family is not opposed to it, they may enjoy learning more about different religions of the world as well.

Imaginational play and creativity

Children who are gifted tend to have great imaginations and they utilize them for play and for explaining the world around them. When they are held back and made to express their abilities only in academic formats, without room for creativity or use of their imaginations, they may become less and less creative and may even become depressed or lethargic (Vaivre-Douret, 2011, https://www.hindawi.com/journals/ijpedi/2011/420297/#B57).

The more that parents can encourage preschool children to use their imaginations and be creative, the less likely their children will take on negative self-image issues, such as what Vaivre-Douret (2011) describes as "narcissistic withdrawal, behavioural deviance, and even personality problems (such as substance abuse disorders) or later decompensation episodes, in particular during adolescence, in the form of aggressiveness tending towards delinquency or depressive states accompanied by suicidal attitudes, and so forth." These concerns are serious and if a child seems to be less excited about learning, the parent or caretaker can add more creative outlets and opportunities for them to use their imaginations, and perhaps their interest in the project will improve, as will their whole demeanor (and possibly with long-term effects!)

Create play and learning environments

Find ways to create an environment that encourages the gifted preschool aged child to explore and create. Allow them a space in the house that they can have books and art materials available and encourage them to use the materials by giving them fun ideas to do. Creating a "maker space," where the child can build structures or use recycled materials will encourage engineering skill building and personal social-emotional skills such as perseverance and trial-and-error. Allowing them to help decorate the space will promote ownership and excitement about using it, and your child may have good ideas for what they want to use or where they want to put things so as to practice organization and management of resources.

Outdoor play areas that are created for them to explore, swing, climb and run around on are also great places for them to practice large motor skills and gifted preschoolers need to especially be encouraged to run and play, since this age tends to be an age of fine motor work and with the emphasis on academic learning starting around this age, they need to still have plenty of time to be physically active.

Working on social skills

There are a lot of references to social-emotional skills in reference to gifted children because the gifted often have different intensities and reactions to situations that make social-emotional skill development particularly helpful and important, especially in the younger ages. There are resources available for teaching social skills, but it is important that whatever route parents and other educators take with developing these skills, that they keep in mind the unique traits of the gifted, rather than just trying to find generic character building types of curriculum or materials. Some basic social skills that can be worked on at the preschool age were listed by Requarth (1992, Creating a Nurturing Classroom Environment, http://files.eric.ed.gov/fulltext/ED347752.pdf), as being "values for living":

1. Appreciating and respecting leaders, family and friends

2. Seeing through the eyes of others and having compassion for their views, growing in sensitivity, acceptance, and concern for their well-being

3. Developing skills in building relationships and communicating effectively

4. Pursing and expressing positive attitudes, thoughts, and actions

5. Understanding personal worth and value

6. Recognizing and developing unique individual abilities and sharing them freely with others

7. Building confidence and enjoying self-expression

8. Channeling energies, developing self-discipline with a realization of natural consequences

9. Establishing goals, and implementing plans

10. Handling stress caused by frustrations, problem, and mistakes

11. Accepting responsibility and meeting deadlines, developing an awareness of standards and obligations in life

12. Making effective use of time

13. Becoming independent in learning, developing an inward motivation to pursue learning experiences

You may notice a similarity between this list of values and the different categories for executive functions (that we discuss in chapter 15). These are skills that can be discussed and worked on throughout the daily activities with your gifted preschooler. The more familiar they are with these phrases and concepts, the more likely they will be comfortable working on them as they enter their school-aged years and classes in the future.

12

School readiness issues

Kindergarten readiness

Young gifted children may need additional support when making the transition into the K-12 school system due to the likelihood that they are academically advanced in comparison to their same-aged peers, and due to potential social-emotional characteristics such as asynchronous development that may cause them to act less mature. It is important that parents visit the schools, preview the classrooms, and talk with the teachers and administrators. Kindergarten programs vary in quality, in class sizes, in resources available for learning, teacher personalities and more.

Start investigating your options for kindergarten early, and when you know for sure what program or school your child will attend, use the time during the year prior to enrollment to prepare your child for the idea and procedures related to going to school. Just as preparing for other transitions, such as going to preschool, the child will be more at-ease with the process if it is something they have had time to think about, talk about and hopefully even visit. The more they are familiar with school type activities, the better, such as lining up to walk as a group, raising their hand to talk in class discussions, taking turns, sharing materials, and even using materials such as small tables and desks, scissors, packets of crayons, lined paper and more.

Young gifted children may have more anxiety about kindergarten than other children, because it is a huge step towards greater independence and represents a wealth of learning opportunities, as well as it represents a huge change and many gifted children struggle with change and transitions. You may see more acting out and regression during this period prior and right after starting kindergarten. And once they are attending classes regularly, you may see their attitudes change—if they were dreading the change, they may find it was less scary than they anticipated; or if they were excited about it and built it up in their minds as being an amazing experience to attend kindergarten and they find it is less exciting, they may be less eager to attend. Continuing to discuss the ups and downs and reassure them, while also addressing any real areas of concern with their teachers and/or administration as necessary, will help them feel supported and hopefully make their first year of formal instruction a successful time.

Acceleration

Some young gifted children need alternative educational opportunities due to high academic abilities. Acceleration does not always mean grade-skipping and could instead be one or a combination of many different other options, including subject area acceleration, compacting, differentiation, online programs, and combinations of these. The options, however, could be limited by the school or district's policies and available services and the expertise and training of the staff and administrators. Also, keep in mind that any decision to accelerate should be done based on hard evidence, not only the opinions of the people involved. This means looking at what specific and measurable needs the child has, what available options there are to meet those needs (or how the current acceleration options could be tailored to work for the child's needs), and then continuing to monitor the child's progress to ensure continued success (to make sure the student is able to successfully participate in the option that was chosen, or whether the child needs further acceleration than what was already done).

Subject area acceleration

Students who excel in one, or even a few subject areas may benefit from going to other classrooms for instruction at a higher level in that/those areas. This is less of a complete change for a student who may want to stay with their friends in their age-level classroom, but still provides a higher level of curriculum. The downside to this option is that the new classroom may still not move at a fast-enough pace and once they get used to the new environment they could get bored or frustrated if they are ready to move at a quicker pace. The teachers and/or administrators may feel that the subject acceleration was a sufficient accommodation and may not think the child needs additional support unless the child or parent advocates for additional changes.

Monitoring the success of this type of acceleration is an ongoing process and the whole team should continue to work together to find a good academic fit for the child. Usually when this type of accommodation is agreed to, it is after data review and the team of parents, teacher/s, administrators and possibly school counselors or psychologists meeting to discuss the options. During the meeting when the acceleration is agreed to, the team can discuss how they will continue to monitor the child's success into the future.

Compacting and differentiation

Teachers can provide subject area acceleration in the general education classroom, so that the child does not have to leave their regular location. But that entails some extra work for the teacher, at least on the front end of the plan. Teachers can work with students to create a compacted plan for achievement—allowing the child to work more quickly through the curriculum materials, or to test out of having to do the daily work with the class. This type of learning requires the teacher to differentiate instruction, meaning that she or he provides different curriculum or lessons to different students, or allows a variety of products to be created so that children work on the skills they need to work on, even if the class is all discussing the same theme or topic. Differentiation can be done by offering different types of content or process as well, meaning that the teacher could offer different types of lessons on different topics, or they could allow students to work in different ways on the same lessons.

There are many ways that a teacher can provide individualized instruction to different students, although teachers often have limited time and have a lot of other pressures on them to move through the curriculum at a set pace, and to show mastery of the whole class at the same time, so differentiation is difficult. It is even more difficult when a class has multiple levels of students with differing needs. However, when done well, differentiation is a way to meet the needs of different students while allowing them to stay in the same classroom location together.

Online programs

With advances in technology and a market developing with many options of online programs, education in the online realm has grown. Children, including young learners are able to access a variety of learning materials. They can take a formal class here or there, or even supplement their classroom work with videos or other tutorials if they need more information or examples about something they are learning about. It is also possible for K-12 children to do all of their learning online now, with states offering virtual school experiences and other companies seeing a niche for them to also provide curriculum programs. Students who need an accelerated course can take online classes at home or at school, and still take other courses with their friends. When they are older, they can even take college courses online while they are in middle and high school (something to keep in mind for later!).

Online learning is also a valuable way to supplement the preschool or homeschool learning experience and a fun way for kids to increase their technology skills, which will be more and more valuable in their future.

Kindergarten early-entrance

Some states do not allow early-entrance to kindergarten, but if your child has the option there are many things that should be looked it. Most importantly, if a child is academically ready to attend kindergarten and is not quite at the state required attendance age, then parents need to find out what rules apply and then evaluate whether their child would benefit from any other options or if kindergarten entrance would be best. The rules for kindergarten entry vary from state to state. You can find your state's kindergarten rules at this link: http://www.ecs.org/state-kindergarten-policies-state-profiles/.

Reasons that young children may benefit from early entrance to kindergarten include:

-a need to keep learning interesting and not too remedial (so it is not boring)

-a need for further socialization and structured learning environment than preschool may provide

-a need for a safe environment that allows for further support for their academic needs, especially if the child is in an unsafe place otherwise

-a need for access to advanced learning opportunities beyond the kindergarten curriculum

Boredom is a factor that should not be underrated in it's potential to damage a child's achievement. Research shows that when a student is bored, their brain's emotional filter, the amygdala, can block learning.

According to Dr. Judy Willis, author of *Inspiring Middle Schools Minds*, "If learning opportunities are not compatible with a gifted child's level of intelligence, background knowledge, and development, his brain drops into a stress reactive state. This part of the brain functions at the reactive, involuntary, unconscious level. The brain's only options at this operating level are fight/flight/freeze, which manifests with reactions such as low participation, failure to complete homework and other assignments, disruptive behavior, or simply zoning out (and sometimes missing important material because their brains are no longer paying attention)." (Boredom is a Brain Turnoff, http://www.greatpotentialpress.com/authors/author-articles/boredom-is-a-brain-turn-off)

Gifted students who are more advanced than the learning experiences being presented to them can become bored, which then means they use their energy in different ways—often talking with other students, playing around or zoning out, and then they are flagged by teachers for less positive reasons and may begin a pattern of negative behaviors at school.

Another reason to consider acceleration for young children who are gifted is so as to avoid allowing the child to get into a different sort of pattern of behavior—that of believing that school should be easy, and that if they are as "smart" as people have told them they are, that anything that is not easy is evidence of them not being smart anymore. Children who enter school and things come so easy for them end up not learning executive function skills that would help them later when school becomes more difficult. Usually these students seem to skate through school with ease for many years, not having to put much effort into what they do, and not having to ask for assistance or take notes. Then in about the middle school or high school years, or even college, the student encounters concepts that they are not familiar with, or multi-step problems that require them to write things down and analyze different parts of the issue, and then they freeze and do not have the necessary coping skills that they would have had, if they had struggled earlier in their educational careers. They may exhibit delaying tactics or try to avert the attention of their educators and parents by creating other scenarios such as getting kicked out of the classroom or being sick to their stomachs.

Some gifted students may be rejected by their like-age peers and may do better with older children. Bailey et al. (2004) suggests that "Judgments about the student's social and emotional maturity should include input from the student's parents/care takers and the psychologist. Gifted students are sometimes rejected by their classmates. It is important that teachers do not confuse the absence of close peer relationships with social immaturity." (Types of acceleration and their effectiveness. In Core Module 6: Developing programs and provisions for gifted students. In Stan Bailey, Miraca Gross, Bronwyn MacLeod, Graham Chaffey, Ruth Targett and Caroline Merrick. Professional Development Package for Teachers in Gifted Education. Canberra, Australia: Department of Education, Science and Training.)

It is important that all students be challenged and learn new things every day, so that they do not waste valuable years sitting in classes, learning about things they already know or practicing skills they have already mastered. Early entrance to kindergarten is one potential type of acceleration that helps kick off their school experience on a challenging note, rather than a passive one.

That being said, there are many reasons NOT to enroll a child early in formal education or to pursue acceleration. Some children have gaps in their knowledge that need to be filled before they can be successful at the next level of independence or the next grade. These gaps may be easily filled, and it does not make sense to take more time reviewing materials than they actually need (some children may need only one lesson on a skill they are missing, before they are able to use that skill independently; while some need more review). Acceleration could happen at the same time that gaps are being filled, but this will take careful choreography by the teacher and/or parents, so as to not move too quickly to new materials while they still are experiencing frustration with necessary components, and so they don't skip over things by acting like they understand things that they do not understand. This is one of the reasons why acceleration needs to be done based on actual hard data, rather than just opinions—sometimes we miss things because gifted kids are good at making us think they know things that they may only superficially understand.

Some children also may not have the necessary motor skills, and an additional year of school or more time practicing those skills with their same-aged peers may help them mature enough physically to participate with their classmates. This is not to say that twice exceptional students should not have access to education whenever they are ready for it, or that physical mobility issues should be a reason to exclude a child from learning opportunities, this is just one of the reasons some parents wait until their child is at the same age as their peers when they enter kindergarten, or pursue other forms of acceleration. This also may have to do with future sports participation issues, when smaller size or motor skills may impact competitiveness … but that's a different topic!

Some children are not emotionally ready to attend school early and be away from their parents and may need an additional year to prepare for that scenario. And some children need more down time, such as naps or quiet activities, while they are in their preschool ages, than what kindergarten or higher grade levels provide.

Another issue that has been at the forefront of discussions about kindergarten lately, is that schools have pushed testing and test-preparation practice activities into the lower grades and even into kindergarten in the last decade or so. This means that kindergarten is no longer the place where children learn through play, as much as they are expected to meet (sometimes stringent) academic standards and perform with paper and pencil in desks much more than they had to do in the past. Research is mixed about the impacts of pushing such young children to do what some perceive as non-age-appropriate learning in the younger ages. Therefore, parents should visit kindergarten programs and classrooms and discuss the expectations and format of the programs with the teachers and administrators before making a decision about what age the child should enter kindergarten, and what program, school, or classroom is the best fit.

Possible types of gifted support services/programs in K-12 school

Kindergarten may or may not have gifted services, depending on state laws and program structures. If they do not have formal gifted services, then it is important to look for the following types of characteristics that work best for gifted children:

- -self-regulated pacing (Montessori, flexible groupings, low student/teacher ratios to enable more individualized support)
- -social skills focused (without being just a canned program)
- -teacher with gifted training (or endorsement)
- -other gifted children (but not necessarily ALL gifted children, or even formally identified gifted)
- -arts and creativity based
- -play time and relaxation time

If the kindergarten does offer a formal gifted program, you should look at what kinds of options they have and then find the one that best suits your child's needs. It is likely the school will only have one format available at the kindergarten level, but if they offer more than one then you may have a choice. Keep in mind that even if the program is set in stone as to what the format is, parents and other team members can help create an education plan that may add more accommodations or flexibility into your child's day, which may help adapt the program to fit individualized needs.

When considering a formal gifted program for the kindergarten year, look for the same things above, plus consider the following (if they are choices you can consider at your child's school):

Pull out programs

Gifted programs that occur when a child is removed from their regular general education classroom and then given projects or social activities to do in another location are considered pull-out programs. The benefit of this type of program is that it can occur in coordination with the child still being a part of their general education class, which means they do not have to leave friends to go to a completely different classroom or school full-time. But it also means that the services are limited to usually one or a couple sessions per week for a limited amount of time, and the child is likely not supported by a gifted education trained teacher in the general education classroom the rest of the week.

This format works well for high achievers who enjoy their general education classroom, or classrooms where the teacher and the child genuinely respect and enjoy each other, so the child enjoys remaining in the general education classroom. It also is a way that a child whose cultural identity is supported better by remaining in their home neighborhood and who may not want to have to be in a fulltime program.

On the other hand, students and teachers often complain that the pull-out model requires the student to catch up with general education classroom activities and that the enrichment work that occurs in the gifted pull-out room may not align well with the learning goals that are required of students in the regular classroom, so it may amount to more work for the gifted student, or at least breaks in their day that may make it harder to feel included in some activities (especially when the activities are enjoyable, such as when teachers do games or other fun events when the gifted child is out of the classroom).

Immersion and clustering

Students who remain in their general education classroom fulltime, with a gifted education trained teacher who differentiates instruction so that the child receives the support he or she needs are often the students who have the best of all worlds. They can stay with their friends and neighbors without being pulled out of the room. They can use curriculum compacting if they need acceleration, and they can work with students of all abilities, so they improve social skills with real world application to many different types of social situations.

This type of service format works best for gifted students when they are clustered with other gifted students in the classroom so they have more likelihood of making true peer friendships. It also works best when the teacher honestly enjoys working with gifted students and is able to make them feel challenged and engaged by effective differentiation and novelty through project-based learning. This type of service format does not work well if the gifted student feels stressed by not having enough teacher support because the teacher is stretched too thin and does not manage the differentiation well (it is a difficult task to balance a five ring circus in the classroom all the time!), or if the student still does not feel adequately challenged or supported. This approach requires a lot of administration and parent support, and much planning at the beginning (but then it can run smoothly once the procedures are put in place and the student and teacher fall into a rhythm).

Full-day academically advanced/accelerated classroom

Some gifted programs offer a full-day option where gifted students attend class together in one room and do accelerated curriculum. This format allows gifted children to work on challenging projects together and get to know each other, with the idea that they will form closer peer relationships with others that are similar to them. The problem with this format is that there is an assumption that just because the students are all formally labeled as gifted, that they will all have similar interests, motivation levels and academic abilities. Sometimes schools remove students from the gifted program altogether if they cannot keep up with the advanced instruction and acceleration, even when they are gifted and happen to be underperforming for any of multiple reasons.

A side note: This format works well for students who are high achievers, and often high achieving students who do not have other gifted characteristics or needs are put into these classrooms, sometimes because the gifted evaluations allow for it, sometimes because parents push for it and find loopholes for their students to attend, based on a belief that the program will offer better learning opportunities for their children. Often those students will appear to excel in this type of program because the focus is on high achievement, not necessarily any other gifted traits. Or if it is a program based on gifted characteristics and needs such as high level divergent thinking and social-emotional skill building, those nongifted high achievers may not feel they fit in, or may not perform as well as their parents hope.

Another problem with this format is that gifted children are not expected to work with students who are nongifted, which can create an elitist atmosphere and students may not learn skills that are important for them to use to work with people of diverse abilities in the future. This format also does not work well if the curriculum is not further adapted for gifted children, beyond just being accelerated. And if this type of program does not offer support for underachievers to also succeed, then many gifted students may choose to leave the program because they can't catch up or succeed under the pressure.

Full-day personalized instruction with integrated academics/ acceleration as needed

There are also full-day gifted programs that are not acceleration based. These classrooms offer more of a differentiated approach to learning, including project-based learning and curriculum compacting as needed. This way students who are gifted but are not high performing in every subject area can still succeed. Usually the focus in this type of classroom is on supporting gifted characteristics and needs, especially the social-emotional skill building that young gifted children need to work on.

The main drawbacks to this type of program format are that students often must be bussed to a central location for this type of program to include gifted children from across the region. And that requires that the children leave their home schools and do not often have much interaction with their nongifted (or non-formally-identified) friends.

Acceleration

Some schools consider acceleration such as grade skipping or subject skipping (and Advanced Placement, International

Baccalaureate or dual enrollment at the older grades) to be gifted education support. This is not necessarily true. Sure, any class can be differentiated for gifted students if a gifted education trained teacher is facilitating the instruction. But acceleration is only one type of accommodation for gifted children and should not be a "program option" on its own. Gifted students who are in need of acceleration should still be provided additional support for their other characteristics and needs.

2e services

Gifted children who are twice exceptional will have additional services available to them that should be adapted to work with gifted services as well. Parents of 2e children should request that the gifted coordinator at the school, or at least a teacher with gifted education training or a gifted endorsement, be able to attend IEP meetings so as to ensure that the student receives gifted services in addition and in coordination with their other special education accommodations and support.

Educator responsibilities to keep in mind for any program option

The National Joint Committee on Learning Disabilities provides a list of traits that educators and instructors providing services to young children with special needs should have, and it works great for supporting gifted students as well as twice exceptional students. Professionals providing support to these children should be able to:

- Work well with families,

- provide culturally and linguistically sensitive services,

- promote interagency coordination,

- engage in professional collaboration,

- advocate for matching the needs of individual children to a continuum of available services and supports

- possess knowledge and skills related to both typical and atypical child developmental patterns in domains such as cognition, communication, emergent literacy, motor and sensory function, social–emotional adjustment, and academic development

(NJCLD, 1997/2001d, 1999/2001e,
(http://www.ldonline.org/article/11511/)

Achievement vs. underachievement

Although gifted students have the potential to achieve at high levels, not all of them do so for a variety of reasons. In fact, Weis (1972) stated that over half of gifted students will not perform to their potential. The word potential is problematic when talking about gifted children because we really have no way of measuring their top potential. Even when they take IQ tests, we can only measure as high as they achieve on that one test. It is difficult to score high on those tests, but very easy to score lower than your true potential. Depending on the child's attitude, demeanor and a variety of other variables, a child could score different points on different IQ tests, even when the same instrument is utilized. So it is important that we not create a bar for achievement that they must shoot for, but that we instead light a fire of interest in learning that allows them to compete with themselves and continuously improve their skills.

Achievement vs. underachievement impacts

Some of the environmental and personal factors that may contribute to a gifted child academically achieving or underachieving are the following:

Advantages

Some children have opportunities that allow them more practice with learning and the skills that contribute to success in academics. For example, children who come from homes that have books in them and have parents or caretakers who can read to them when they are small, and who have money to travel and provide extracurricular experiences that families without those opportunities may not experience. Whether a child has advantages such as these in their lives may impact whether the child is able to do better on certain academic requirements and may impact what children appear to be doing better in school than others (even if they are no different in natural intellect to begin with).

Motivation

Students who are motivated because they enjoy the materials that are being studied, or they have strong self-confidence related to their potential success in the class or on that activity, or who just enjoy learning and doing the assigned tasks, will appear to be higher achievers than students who may not be as motivated. Some students come to school with other concerns at home or trauma in their lives and they may not be as motivated to learn.

Interests

Student interest varies depending on what is being studied, as well as what they could be doing if they were home that day (such as being aware that they are missing interacting with their parent who is home while they are at school, or wanting to go outside for recess but they are required to do something else in the classroom, etc.). Students who are interested in learning about what is being presented are much more likely to achieve on related tasks than those who are less interested. Teachers and parents can increase a child's interest in a topic by connecting it with something the child enjoys (such as talking about soccer games that people play in

other countries, if the child loves soccer, and then connecting that
with finding the country on the map...).

Relationships and personalities

If students feel connected to the people they are in the classroom
or other learning environment with, they are much more likely to
enjoy being there. If a gifted child senses that their teacher is
annoyed with them or that other children do not want to work with
them, then they are not as likely to achieve on tasks that require
them to be in that environment. It is important that teachers and
parents and students work on social-emotional support issues so
that the children feel safe in the classroom and are happy to be
there and feel respected by others.

Belief systems

Some families hold education up high as something that is
considered important. They may talk about their children going to
college someday, and expect that their children do well in school.
Some family members may have had negative school experiences
and they do not feel as excited about school situations. Depending
on the beliefs about education in the home, and the child's own

beliefs about education mattering, a child may be more or less likely to achieve. It is important for educators and parents to confront these types of personal beliefs in their own thoughts so that they can help the children have positive learning experiences.

Skills and challenge/struggle

Some gifted students will be naturally drawn to certain types of learning. For example, some have more abilities in math than in language arts, and vice versa. However, even naturally talented students need to refine their skills. The more confident a child is with his or her skills in an academic area, the more likely they are to achieve. It is important that people working with gifted children not assume that they already have skills unless there is evidence of achievement that shows that the skills are mastered. Sometimes people think that being gifted means that all skills will come naturally, but gifted children should acquire new skills on a regular basis if they are appropriately placed in challenging academic classes and levels. They should be encouraged to find a balance between using some skills they are comfortable with, and trying new things so as to learn new skills. This balance creates confidence and a comfort with trying new things that will help the child achieve.

The more parents and educators are aware of these impacts on achievement, the more they can watch the gifted children to ensure they are on-track and moving forward in their learning without issues.

Homeschool vs. private vs. public school options

Finding the right fit for gifted children in an education system is sometimes a hard thing. Public school districts serve a lot of different children and often their gifted services are comprised only by a "program" that consists of particular classrooms where gifted children participate in curriculum that is still based on the general education program standards but may be accelerated or have a gifted endorsed teacher at the helm. This may or may not be adequate support for a specific child. If your child is not ready to be accelerated at the same pace and level as the others in the classroom in every content area subject, or they are more advanced than the class level allows, they may not feel that the pacing or level is appropriate. Research shows that gifted children are often not talented in every subject area (some gravitate towards logical/sequential types of activities and are more mathematically inclined, and others are more language oriented and do better on reading and writing activities, see

http://journals.sagepub.com/stoken/rbtfl//bwNip9GMWEg2/full).

Students in public schools often spend a lot of time waiting for others to gain the skills needed for the whole class to move on. As Subotnik et al. (2011) states, "Every student in the United States is guaranteed a free and appropriate education, but too many academically gifted students spend their days in school *relearning* material they have already mastered, trapped in classes that are not challenging and too slow paced."
(http://journals.sagepub.com/stoken/rbtfl//bwNip9GMWEg2/full) In order to improve the educational experiences of gifted and other high achieving students, schools often have them attend pull-out or full-time gifted classes that may or may not alleviate this problem of mismatched pacing.

Some states require educational plans (similar to Individualized Education Plans that are required by federal law for other special education students) that spell out specific skills and/or related behaviors and accommodations that a gifted child will work on or receive during the school year. But even those plans are often generic and based on fitting the child to the program, rather than creating education opportunities matched to the child's specific needs. Parents can be part of the educational plan team at the school and can ask that the plans be more specific, while keeping in mind that gifted education is not covered under the same federal law protections that other special education areas are, so enforcement of the plan contents can be difficult. It is best to work as cooperatively with the school team as possible, as they are the people who will ensure that your child is supported more than anything that the plan may state.

Non-public-school options

Because of those reasons above, and sometimes other issues such as conflicts with teachers and administrators, school location, religious beliefs and more, parents sometimes choose to enroll their gifted children in private schools or to take them out of schools completely—providing their education through homeschooling or even unschooling. There are a range of possible options for children, depending on what state they live in (as each state has their own laws and options regarding educational experiences). Some states offer vouchers for students to attend private schools or to access homeschool curriculum materials using tax dollars, and some do not even allow homeschooling. It is up to the parent to research what opportunities are available to their child.

Private schools

Private schools may or may not offer sufficient gifted educational services. Some private schools require their teachers to have extensive training in this area, and some private schools do not even require their teachers to have state teacher certificates. Some private schools offer a range of choices for educational paths and have multiple levels of achievement available for students who are ready for acceleration, and some private schools are behind the public schools in terms of achievement or educational program options. It is important for parents to not only research what is available, but to visit the schools and to discuss gifted issues with the staff. If the staff seems welcoming and informed about gifted issues and is flexible and willing to work with your child's individual personality and needs, that may be a great match. However, if a school program has less flexibility and staff are quick to gloss over or dismiss your concerns about gifted issues, you may be better off looking at other options.

Charter schools

There are also some states that allow charter schools, which are schools that operate as private schools but they partner with the states or districts so they can use state tax money instead of charging tuition. Charter schools often have to follow similar standards as the other public schools, but they may have smaller class sizes or offer specialized programs that the public schools do not offer. Charter schools work with the districts to share responsibility for special services for special education students and sometimes provide gifted support services. Just as parents should check out private schools to ensure adequate services for their gifted children, they should also check out charter schools and not assume that just because they are willing to take your child that your child should attend that school without making sure it will be a good fit.

Homeschool, unschool or hybrid options

Some gifted young children have high energy and/or are not interested in sitting in classrooms where they must raise hands to ask questions and do assigned tasks in a specific order. They may have unique academic needs or struggle behaviorally in a school setting, or they may develop a dislike for education in general in the school system. Yet, those same children may flourish when allowed to learn through less rigid controls, so some parents choose to homeschool their children or to do a hybrid approach, using part time school and part time home activities (such as using an online curriculum program or participating in activities at a brick and mortar school for part of their days). Some families decide to allow their children to learn in nontraditional ways and call their desire to not use a specific curriculum or mandated traditional school activities (but rather use the world as their classroom and allow the child to access learning opportunities through materials and experiences in their homes and on field trips), as "unschooling," which is defined differently by different families, as is the concept of homeschooling in general (which may also look differently in different homes).

Many gifted children thrive in homeschool environments and some choose to return to, or enter, the school system at a later time. Some do all of their K-12th grade age learning through homeschooling and attend college later or obtain careers using their homeschool records. And others may struggle to stay as motivated as their program administrators or parents expect, and other accommodations or arrangements may be made.

Homeschooling offers flexibility that schools may not be able to provide, but it also relies on parents or other caretakers being able to support the legal and personal requirements that districts and children require. Some states require that parents keep a log of activities, and some require proof of adequate progress in the form of testing or teacher evaluation on a regular basis. Parents do not have to be certified teachers in order to guide homeschooling children, but they should have the knowledge and interest in providing flexible academic activities and gifted-specific social-emotional support as needed if they are working with gifted children.

Additional community options

Some communities offer additional support programs or workshops for young children who need additional activities or social-emotional skill building opportunities, such as workshops and cooperative lessons for homeschoolers or gifted support groups where the children can work and play with other kids. Gifted children also often benefit from being involved in team or individual sports that offer practice in additional social skills and allows them to be more physically active (which is something that children need more now that they spend more time sitting and doing more technology-based activities).

Parents of gifted children have more options these days than students of the past, but sometimes those choices are not obvious and not well-advertised. Do not be afraid to ask questions and to be creative in order to piece together the best plan for your child. It is most important that children enjoy learning and continue to use internal motivation in order to achieve. Research has shown that intrinsic motivation and task commitment are two of the most important skills that lead to achievement in education and future careers (Matthews D.J., Foster J.F., 2009, Being Smart about

Gifted Education: A guidebook for educators and parents, 2nd ed.,

Scottsdale, AZ: Great Potential Press; Renzulli J.S., 1986, The

Three-Ring Conception of Giftedness: A developmental model for

creative productivity. In Sternberg R.J., Davidson J.E., (Eds.),

Conceptions of Giftedness, New York, NY: Cambridge University

Press).

Finding educational experiences that challenge and interest young

gifted children and prepare them for their futures is not easy and

parents should look toward their team that they have been working

with during their child's birth through preschool years in order to

bounce ideas off them and look for additional information and

emotional support.

What educational programs does our school/district provide for gifted students?

Name of school (preschool, elementary, middle school, high school, private, charter, public, etc.)	Does the school offer pull-out gifted services, full-time gifted classes, or immersion classes?	Does the school offer twice exceptional support by gifted-trained educators/ professionals?	What types of acceleration or other academic supports do they offer?

13

Additional at-risk issues for gifted children

Underachievement

Gifted students who underperform in academics are at-risk of other social-emotional issues. They may stress or have depression issues. They also may gravitate towards other underperformers and could be at risk of behaviors that could get them into trouble at school, home and in the community. A lot of times underperforming gifted students are lacking motivation, but if they continue to underperform they may begin missing out on skill building that other students are learning.

Therefore, we need to consider both students who are underperforming because things are too hard, as well as too easy.

These gifted children all need the following support in order to get back on track and find the right academic fit:

- Teachers who are trained in gifted characteristics and needs.
- Counseling support for potential frustrations, anxiety, depression regarding changes in their academic placement and peer issues.
- Acceleration as needed, but also time to review skills in a respectful and engaging manner (if in group situations—with other bright students).
- Possibly a new peer group (these students may still need acceleration in some subject areas, and may still need time with gifted peers in a gifted class—pull out or full time).
- Novelty—things that are interesting to the student and new things to think about.
- Challenge based on things that they are curious about or compelled to participate in.

Underperforming students may have the following characteristics that need support:

- Low self-perceived academic abilities

- Negative attitudes toward school, teachers, and/or classes

- Poor self-management/low motivation

- Socially immature, lacking self-discipline

- Unpopular/few friends

- Resistant to influence from teachers or parents

- May become withdrawn in classroom situations

(From Davis, 2005, and Delisle and Galbraith, 2002, found at https://www.youtube.com/watch?v=MFUQiXADdkQ.)

Dr. Sylvia Rimm (ND) found that underachieving gifted students are often disorganized, dawdle, forget homework, lose assignments and misplace books; and that they daydream, talk too much to other children, have poor study skills—or none at all, have innumerable excuses and defenses, and think school is boring when they are young, irrelevant when they are older (http://www.sylviarimm.com/newsletters/Newsletter%2019.1.pdf). These are all reasons that gifted children need to be supported starting at a very young age, so that they do not develop habits related to underachievement. And when parents or teachers do notice a pattern of underperforming, they should take it seriously and work to alleviate the causes so that the child does not fall farther and farther behind.

Misbehavior

Some gifted children act out with inappropriate behavior when they are frustrated with their abilities or they feel like there is a misfit with their placement. They also may try new behaviors in order to manipulate situations or to get attention.

Gifted children who try the limits and boundaries of authority and the rules of their environments may be at-risk for being tracked into programs for behavioral issues or may isolate themselves from others who do not want to be involved in their disobedience. Gifted kids are not only good at pushing the buttons of people they want to get a rise out of, but they also are clever at ways to get into trouble if they decide to go that route. This quote sums up the gifted child's ability to choose to use their brilliance in negative manners:

> "Everybody has known at least one, that exceptionally bright child that constantly got in trouble and refused to behave. I'm referring to the clever one that knows how to "crack" the

computer codes, repair the laptop and build rockets, but instead blows up the school toilet. Many gifted children misbehave."

(Neglect, Boredom, Curiosity, Sibling Rivalry, and Peer pressure, http://www.helium.com/items/1110528-problem-children.)

Gifted children may not mean to get themselves into situations, but their emotional intensities may amplify their response when they do not get their way, or they are trying to be creative in obtaining attention. This potential knack for causing chaos may create stress at home and in school. "Being gifted does not mean that the child should be intelligent enough not to misbehave. What it does mean is that, when gifted children do misbehave, the misbehavior is more diverse and more amplified than with a mainstream child." (http://www.muffledvoices.info/2013/04/gifted-mischief.html.)

If a gifted child is heading down the wrong path, the first route of trying to avert trouble should be talking with them. Usually they are able to use empathy or other logic to understand that they are making poor choices. However, for children who insist on getting into trouble repeatedly, parents and caregivers may want to investigate what else is triggering this behavior. Sometimes it has to do with the child feeling stress about something else—perhaps their progress in school is problematic and they need help; or they are having issues with bullies; or they need help working through their emotional response to other environmental concerns such as awareness of parental strife. It also could be something serious such as substance abuse in the family or other types of child abuse or neglect.

On the other hand, they just may think that getting negative attention is fun, or the challenge of breaking rules is exciting. When a gifted child is struggling with misbehavior, it is important to take it seriously and help them get back to where they need to be in terms of attitude and surround them with care and support so they do not slip further and cause themselves more trouble, as misbehavior can have serious consequences including underachievement, loss of learning time and opportunities, and even criminal implications.

Gender issues

Lynn Rose (1999) (University of Connecticut,

http://nrcgt.uconn.edu/newsletters/spring994/) found that girls may

receive less encouragement to be involved with math and science

from parents and teachers, starting at early ages. Historically

parents did not buy as many mathematical skill-based toys for girls

as they did for boys, and girls were not encouraged as much to see

themselves as mathematically talented. Now, since the Women's

Rights Movement and other improvements in identifying that

females need to be more encouraged to achieve in the science and

math fields, and according to Kerr (2000), "efforts to create

programs to encourage gifted girls to greater aspirations and

achievement have proliferated. The programs have been so

successful that gifted girls now have aspirations very similar to

gifted boys throughout high school, and even spend more time and

effort planning their careers than boys."

That being said, we still have to keep in mind to not restrict

achievement in any gender. Play objects that encourage logic skill

building and other scientific thinking should be available for males

and females.

Males have other types of pressures, for example society may give them messages about having to be "macho" and may make them think that certain things they want to do are less desirable for boys to do because they were labeled as not very masculine, such as play with dolls or wear pink. But gifted children often explore all sorts of concepts and do not like being limited by the rules of society. They need to know it is fine and even desirable for them to play as if they are parenting, and that they can wear whatever colors or play with whatever toys they want to play with.

There are resources available to read more about gender issues and gifted children and if your child is struggling with issues related to their gender it may be a good idea to discuss the issues with your team including counselors familiar with this type of thing. If your child seems to be bullied over gender expression, contact school administrators as soon as possible so this is stopped and students are educated on issues so as to spread support for your child among compassionate friends.

Many gifted children have androgynous traits, due to not wanting to conform to gender-role stereotypes (Sheely, A. R. (2000). Sex and the highly gifted adolescent. *Highly Gifted Children Newsletter,* 13(2), 30-33. The Hollingworth Center for Highly Gifted Children), and rejecting strict gender identities (Tolan, S. S. (1997). Sex and the highly gifted adolescent. *Counseling and Guidance*, 6(3), 2, 5, 8. Retrieved March 25, 2012, from http://www.stephanietolan.com/hg_adolescent.htm).

Gifted children are likely to explore gender identity issues, starting at a young age. According to Wexelbaum and Hoover (2014), "for developmental reasons, GTC (gifted, talented and creative program) teachers should assume that their students may question and explore their sexual orientation and/or gender identity earlier than do non-GTC students," and that educators should "assume that a proportion of your GTC students will also identify as LGBTIQ (Lesbian, Gay, Bisexual, Transgendered, Intersex, or Queer)."

Parents and teachers will need to provide additional support for children who may struggle with gender identity issues, and ensure they are in safe environments where they can continue to grow and achieve with peers who accept them and do not cause harm. Professional team members such as counselors and psychologists can help children, families and others to understand and work on any concerns or challenges surrounding gender identity issues.

Notes about at-risk issues

Record any thoughts or resources you have after reading this chapter and/or doing more research on these issues:

14

Parenting gifted young children

As a parent of gifted children there are some specific issues that may come up while parenting gifted young children that should be of particular concern, starting even at birth with prenatal care, and then extending to the ways we play and read with our children and even help them make good ethical choices. The more parents can surround themselves with support from others, the more they can stay the strong role models that gifted children need to thrive.

Prenatal care

Prenatal care is extremely important for the proper development of all babies. Research has shown that mothers who receive regular prenatal care stand a much better chance of delivering healthy, full-term, normal-weight babies than mothers who do not (Carnegie Corporation of New York. (1994) Starting Points, Meeting the Needs of Our Youngest Children). And children with extremely low birth weight score much lower on academic tests than other children.

Pamele Kato Klebonov (1994) states, "as birth weight decreases, the prevalence of grade failure, placement in special classes, and classification as handicapped increases…. ELBW children score lower than all other birth weight groups on math and reading achievement tests. Even among children with IQ scores above 85, ELBW children still obtain lower math scores than normal birth weight children." (School Achievement and Failure in Very Low Birth Weight Children, http://journals.lww.com/jrnldbp/Abstract/1994/08000/School_Achiev ement_and_Failure_in_Very_Low_Birth.5.aspx.)

About 70% of extremely preterm or extremely low birth weight children have cognitive, behavioral or educational disabilities when evaluated at 8 years of age, and nearly 50% exhibit multiple areas of concern. (Esther Hutchinson et al,, School-age Outcomes of

Extremely Preterm or Extremely Low Birth Weight Children, 2013,

http://pediatrics.aappublications.org/content/131/4/e1053.long?tren

dmd-

shared=0&utm_source=TrendMD&utm_medium=TrendMD&utm_ca

mpaign=Pediatrics_TrendMD_0.)

All of these facts point to the importance of prenatal care, so as to

preserve a child's potential for healthy development and to not

harm a gifted child before they even can express their gifted traits.

That being said, infants who were born after compromised prenatal

care may still do well and could still be gifted. It is important though,

as we are discussing gifted infants and babies to point out how

important good prenatal care is, and that parents should start good

habits of parenting, as much as possible even before their children

are born.

Play

Parents and caretakers of gifted children should talk with them

often so as to grow their vocabulary and support their social-

emotional growth. As Fowler (1993) identified, "verbal mastery,

when cognitively based, opens the door to representing,

understanding and able negotiating with knowledgeable older persons to constantly expand one's knowledge and advance one's skills."

But playing with children is just as important for their development. Fowler (1993) also found that parents who played with their kids and used language that was simplified and presented in forms highly accessible and engaging to the child amounted to advanced cognitive skills as reflected in IQ scores and observations of the children's every day competencies, not in just language competencies alone. (The Long-Term Development of Giftedness and High Competencies in Children Enriched in Language during Infancy, at http://files.eric.ed.gov/fulltext/ED358949.pdf.)

Also, Fowler (1993) discovered that when the play and talking was highly socially oriented, involving the child's interest and attention through social interaction, with the adult and the infant taking turns and fostering autonomy in the child, their children progressed the most in cognitive skill building. (This was also supported by a study by Ogston, K. (1983), The effects of gross motor and language stimulation on infant development. In W. Fowler ed., Potentials of

Childhood. vol. 2. Lexington, MA: Lexington Books.)

Bergen (1998) states this well, saying "play is "a major means by

which children's development and learning are initiated and through

which development is achieved and learning is mastered." (Intro,

Play as a Medium for Learning and Development,

http://files.eric.ed.gov/fulltext/ED421252.pdf.)

Spodek and Saracho (1998) held the following, regarding the

reasons that play is important during development:

> Arousal-seeking theory suggests that human beings
>
> normally need to be continually involved in information-
>
> processing activities. The absence of stimuli in a person's
>
> environment will cause discomfort, leading the individual to
>
> increase the amount of perceptual information available,
>
> either by seeking it externally, or by creating it internally. Too
>
> much stimulation will cause individuals to "turn off" their
>
> environments by attending less. Play is a vehicle through

which children mediate the amount of stimulation available to them in order to achieve an optimal arousal level.

(The Challenge of Educational Play, Play as a Medium for Learning and Development.)

When parents are able to not only play with their gifted children they are encouraging thought processes that will help them develop their cognitive abilities for far into the future. Parents can find opportunities for organized play by contacting their local community centers, YMCAs, and looking for local activities advertised through local social networking pages and parent support groups. The more children are exposed to different kind of play, and especially the kinds where there is reciprocity of discussion and connected to real life and social discussions, the more the children will be able to develop concepts and practice skills they will need later in life.

Reading

Throughout the young lives of gifted children, one of the most important skills parents and caretakers can support is the skill of reading. Making books a regular part of our young children's lives will help them associate reading with pleasure, and the more we help them become better readers, the stronger their basic skills will be for a strong foundation of learning.

Perkinson (1996) advises the following:

> Start a home library for them, even if it's just a shelf or two. Be sure to keep some books for little children to handle freely. Consider specially made, extra-durable books for infants, and pick paperbacks and plastic covers for kids who are older but still not quite ready for expensive hardbacks. Allowing little children to touch, smell, and even taste books will help them to develop strong attachments. (Helping Your Child Use the Library, http://files.eric.ed.gov/fulltext/ED400833.pdf.)

The push-pull of the parent/child relationship

Like all children, gifted children rely on family ties being strong enough to keep them safe while they are exploring the world, yet also strong enough to keep them surrounded by love even when they are practicing independence and pushing away. However, with gifted children the attempts at becoming more and more independent start at younger ages and gifted characteristics emphasize the struggle even more. Intense emotional responses create more drama and chaos when gifted children do not have the freedom they desire, yet if they are not given strong boundaries they may react with anxiety and fear about things they are intellectually, but perhaps not emotionally ready for.

Gifted children's outbursts can be intense and they are clever and can push all of our buttons with ease. It is important to keep pulling them back to your side, even while they struggle to explore the world around them. Gifted children may have more experiences with bullying and other peer/friendship struggles, as it is more difficult for them to find other kids like themselves, so they may seem even more lonely at times. Those types of challenges, combined with other identity issues, such as trying to balance gender issues (acting more or less masculine to fit in with peer groups, feeling more or less encouraged to explore interests they have because they are seen as not typical male or female interests, LGBTIQ issues, etc.), and sometimes taking on the weight of the world due to their high emotional responses to empathy situations, make raising gifted children complicated. It is important to keep in mind that the push and pull between parents/caretakers and gifted children are usually normal behaviors and that it is our job to keep them feeling supported, even when they may not be particularly likeable at that moment!

Sibling issues

Being a sibling of a gifted child can also be as difficult as parenting one. However, research shows that often when one child in the family is gifted, other children may be as well. So, having more than one gifted person in the house can exponentially multiply the intensities that gifted children express, so that frustrations and arguments between the siblings are common. It is also possible that one child will have higher abilities or talents than the other, or one could be more skilled with social situations so that they have more friends than the other. It is important to support all children in the home, as well as look at their unique traits and celebrate all of their achievements.

Lying and sneaky stuff

Gifted children may feel compelled to be less than honest at times. Some feel pressure to keep their "smart person" image intact, and cheat on academic assignments or tests. Some are bored in school and entertain themselves by seeing what they can get away with. And some want to do things that are not allowed, and they will go to any ends or means to get there. However, there are other levels of dishonesty as well. As Maupin (2015) states, some gifted children "may have never cheated on a test, or forged a signature or skipped class, but it's almost certain that there has been a time that they have misrepresented themselves in something they have said or done to fit in, or to try to be 'like everyone else.'" (https://educatethebestofme.wordpress.com/2015/04/29/confessions-of-a-gifted-cheater/)

Parents and caretakers should be aware that gifted children are exploring ethical issues, just as other children do in their growing years, but they may have additional pressures on them to lie or cheat. Continue to talk with them about pressures in their lives and talk about values such as honesty so when they do get into a situation where lying or cheating may be tempting, they can balance those pressures with the things you have talked with them about.

Parenting support

Parents who struggle with parenting issues regarding their gifted child/ren are encouraged to join support groups for parents of gifted children. SENG (Supporting Emotional Needs of Gifted, www.sengifted.org) offers SENG Model Parent Group (SMPG) events throughout the country and even the world, where parents can discuss issues that are commonly of importance to parents, facilitated by trained group leaders. And you may be able to find other support groups in your town or region.

Another way to connect with other parents and experts on gifted education is to participate in online networking groups and/or state and national gifted organizations, and to attend gifted education conferences where you can talk with other parents and meet gifted experts in person.

15

Executive functions

Young children need to acquire specific life skills that are often called "executive functions." These skills are the things we need to be able to do in order to organize the things we learn, the things we need to plan and do, and to prioritize activities in our busy lives. Just as many adults struggle to finetune their organization and motivation throughout different life situations, we are never too young to start working on these kinds of things.

The main executive functions we will refer to for this chapter include the following skills:

- **Management of time and resources**

- **Responsibility/self-monitoring**

- **Organization**

- **Impulse/emotional control**

- **Memory**

- **Task initiation/commitment and motivation**

Managing time/resources

Gifted children sometimes struggle with too many thoughts in their minds, so things like managing time and materials and keeping things organized or keeping track of things they need to do are hard to do. There is a saying that someone created into a picture that was posted on social media sometime awhile back, that says something to the effect of that their mind is like a computer with dozens of tabs open at the same time. Life as a gifted person is like that—many tabs open with lots of different things to think about. So, it is important that we help gifted children establish executive function routines that will help them keep track of things they need to do in the future.

Everyone uses executive functions. Even infants and toddlers appreciate a schedule for feedings and naps, which parents help set up and then the babies can count on routines being followed and their bodies adjust to sleep and wake patterns and their stomachs count on food at certain times during the day. Toddlers and preschoolers can start with managing resources by helping pick up toys and put art supplies back where they are supposed to go, so that those materials are available later.

Memory

Young children work on their memory skills from birth, constantly paying attention as infants to things that become familiar—people's faces, locations, pets, toys, etc. They hear songs that they begin to memorize, and the meanings of words. And then as they get older they can remember stories and details and word and number patterns. Gifted children acquire strong memory skills earlier than nongifted children do, and this benefits them when they begin learning even higher-level concepts.

One of the things that comes less naturally for gifted children though, is using memory tools such as note taking and scheduling.

Having young children record things that they learn or draw pictures on a calendar or white board or other location to remind them of what they need to do that day is a good start to practicing note taking and scheduling. Keeping a family diary of fun things you did, in order to remember good times is also a good way to practice using writing or pictures to help remember important things. You can also play games together to see who can remember the most information. Maybe look at a photo of a room and then try to remember all the things that were in the picture. Or give directions and then see if you can remember all the steps.

Impulse/emotion control

It is sometimes difficult for young children to control strong emotions, but life is full of ups and downs that they need to be able to deal with, without falling apart. Talking about different emotions and how to express them in different situations is helpful to gifted youngsters who are trying to figure out how to appropriately express themselves in social situations. Some skills come more naturally after having to use them in real life situations, so exposing young children to real social situations, such as playing at the park or participating in a community center class, etc. is a great way to practice impulse and emotional control skills.

Responsibility/self-monitoring

Young gifted children like to be responsible for important tasks, but they aren't always good at following through. So that is why it is important to give them tasks such as small chores to do around the house, starting when they are very young. Infants who can crawl can usually help throw a toy in a box to help clean up. And toddlers and preschoolers can help with sorting clothes or wiping windows, or even helping set the table or wash dishes. Having important tasks to work on around the house helps them learn how to be responsible and monitor their own progress on the tasks, and it also makes them feel good about contributing around the house.

Organization

Gifted children often need help with organization. Sometimes a young gifted child becomes highly interested in keeping their rooms picked up and having everything in its place, but this is not as usual as gifted children with messy rooms and situations where things they need are hard to find! Working on organizing play areas and keeping clothing sorted are good examples of skill building opportunities for working on organization. Young gifted children often enjoy categorizing, so finding ways that they can categorize their toys and place them on corresponding shelves, or sorting laundry by colors is a good start to finding ways to break larger tasks into smaller ones to make them less intimidating. Having specific places to put important things will help later when children are in school and need to keep track of homework or technology.

Task initiation/commitment and motivation

Many gifted children enjoy trying new things, but then after a few dance lessons or visits to the pool, they may tire of the novelty of the situation and ask to not have to finish the session. This is an example of not having "task commitment." They may have been eager to initiate a new goal, but they did not want to follow through. In order to emphasize commitment and to practice getting through hard spots when things aren't always as fun as a child may think they are supposed to be, parents can encourage children to keep going to classes until they are over or set a goal for trying something new at least a few times before deciding whether it's a good fit.

Some children are not as motivated to try new things or to accomplish goals. This is a problem especially when children who have not been very motivated as preschoolers end up in K-12 educational experiences and they continue to be lazy and unmotivated. It is important that children learn early in life how to make less interesting things palatable—meaning that they be exposed to things that may seem less fun (and even hard work), and that they see parents modeling good attitudes and encouraging them to do a good job even if it is not fun. In this day and age, so many children resort to amusing themselves with electronic games, that they are more likely to be bored out of their minds if they run out of batteries or have to actually participate in something that does not provide instant gratification like video gaming does. The more that young children are encouraged to create their own fun, even during boring or challenging situations, the more they are likely to be able to do the same later in life. Motivation is a key skill for academic success and even career success later in life. The more we can help young children acquire it, the better off they will be long-term.

Executive Functions

According to authors Joyce Cooper-Kahn and Laurie Dietzel, "*The executive functions are a set of processes that all have to do with managing oneself and one's resources in order to achieve a goal. It is an umbrella term for the neurologically-based skills involving mental control and self-regulation.*"
(*www.ldonline.org/article/29122/*)

EXECUTIVE FUNCTION	BASIC DESCRIPTION	HOW ARE YOU ENCOURAGING YOUR CHILD TO GROW IN THIS SKILL AREA?
Managing time and resources/Organization	• Being able to keep track of materials • Paying attention to time limits or at least responding to them appropriately • Being careful with objects and following safety rules	
Responsibility/Self-Monitoring	• Focusing on things they need to do • Listening to directions and following them as appropriate • Being able to look back at how they responded to situations and thinking about consequences (negative and positive)	

Task initiation/Commitment and Motivation	• Knowing when to move to the next task and staying focused on the right things • Not giving up too easily	
Memory	• Being able to remember the things they need to recall • Learning how to take notes or draw pictures to remember things they want to remember	
Impulse/Emotion Control	• Responding appropriately to emotions • Thinking before reacting	

16

Resources for more information

Early Childhood Gifted Issues

Ensign, J., Homeschooling Gifted Students: An Introductory Guide for Parents, http://www.ericdigests.org/1998-2/gifted.htm

Farmer, D. Parenting Gifted Preschoolers, (1996). http://www.davidsongifted.org/Search-Database/entry/A10106

Haensly, P., (2004). Spirit and Opportunity: Re-exploring Giftedness and Parents' Expanding Directive Role http://files.eric.ed.gov/fulltext/EJ684162.pdf

Illinois Council for the Gifted Journal, (1992). This annual issue of the Illinois Council for the Gifted Journal includes 20 articles focusing on young gifted children, http://files.eric.ed.gov/fulltext/ED347752.pdf

Lewis, M., Feiring, C., & McGuffog, C. (1986). Profiles of young gifted and normal children: Skills and abilities are related to sex and handedness. *Topics in Early Childhood Special Education, 6*(1), 9-22.

Lewis, M., & Michalson, L. (1985). The gifted infant. In J. Freeman

(Ed.), *The psychology of gifted children* (pp. 35-57). New York: John Wiley.

Preschool Behaviors in Children, Minnesota Council for the Gifted & Talented, http://mcgt.net/preschool-behaviors-in-gifted-children

Contact links for gifted and twice exceptional organizations

National Association for Gifted Children (NAGC), www.nagc.org

Supporting Emotional Needs of the Gifted (SENG), www.sengifted.org

National Society for the Gifted and Talented (NSGT), https://www.nsgt.org/

World Gifted Council (WGC), https://www.world-gifted.org/

Hoagies Gifted Education Blog (has many other organizations listed and kept up-to-date), http://www.hoagiesgifted.org/organizations.htm

Johns Hopkins University, Center for Talented Youth (CTY), https://cty.jhu.edu/

Gender issues

Kerr, B. (2001). Smart Boys: Talent, Manhood, and the Search for Meaning, https://www.amazon.com/exec/obidos/ASIN/091070743X/thehoagi esgifted/

Kerr, B (2005). Smart Girls: A New Psychology of Girls, Women, and Giftedness (Revised Edition), https://www.amazon.com/exec/obidos/ASIN/091070726X/thehoagi esgifted/

Odean, K (2002). Great Books for Girls: More Than 600 Books to Inspire Today's Girls and Tomorrow's Women,

https://www.amazon.com/exec/obidos/ASIN/0345450213/thehoagie
sgifted/

Pollack, W. (1999). Real Boys: Rescuing Our Sons from the Myths
of Boyhood.
https://www.amazon.com/exec/obidos/ASIN/0805061835/thehoagie
sgifted/.
Wexelbaum, R., Hoover, J. (2014). Gifted and LGBTIQ1: A
Comprehensive Research Review,
http://icieworld.net/en/images/IJTDC%2021%20August%202014.pd
f#page=73

Child Development

Baby's Brain Development During Pregnancy, Raise Smart Kid
blog, at http://www.raisesmartkid.com/pre-natal-to-1-year-old/2-
articles/19-babys-brain-development-during-pregnancy

James and Susie, a gifted allegory, You Tube video:
https://www.youtube.com/watch?v=IIrvZ4fwBKU&noredirect=1

Identifying Advanced Young Children, National Association for
Gifted Children, http://www.nagc.org/resources-
publications/resources-parents/young-gifted-children/identifying-
advanced-young-children

Please also check out my website at

http://oneworldgifted.weebly.com, where you can find more

information about raising and working with gifted children, and my

blog, where I write about gifted issues. Thank you for your interest

in Smart Babies!

— Kathleen Casper

Appendix A

The following pages are summary lists of
potential gifted traits by age group.

Infants

Active more than other babies of similar ages
Early movement skills (moving head, sitting, grasping purposefully)
Early hand-to-eye coordination
Early language acquisition and cognitive processes
Makes eye contact soon after birth and continues interaction and awareness of others
Makes eye contact while nursing
Does not like to be left in infant seat
Almost always want someone in the room interacting with him or her
Very alert
Long attention span
Less need for sleep
Smiling or recognizing caretakers early
Advanced progression through developmental milestones
High activity level
Extraordinary feats of memory

Toddlers

12-18 months
Walking one month earlier than average
Language acquisition 3 1/2 months earlier than average and early acquisition of reading
Obvious interest in competence
Long attention span
Obvious interest in letters, numbers, books, and talking
Surprisingly good eye to hand coordination for shape sorters
Uses puzzles and toys that are beyond stated age level
Does not chew on or tear books
Tries hard to please, feelings easily hurt

Toddlers (continued)

18 to 24 months

Talking, clear understanding of others' talk

Knowing many letters, colors, and numbers, often knowing how to count and organized by quantities, knowing many colors and shades, and knowing the alphabet in order or isolation

Tenacity, needs to do it their own way

Not easily distracted from what they want to do

Notices beauty in nature

Pays attention to the feelings of others

Needs to know why before complying

Can sing a song with you, knows all the words and melody

Clearly exhibits a sense of humor beyond typical bathroom humor

Although active, activity is usually very purposeful and important to them

Interested in activities, machinery, and implements that our complex and maybe delicate

Bossy — loses interest in any children who cannot do what they want to do

Others may complain that your child is willful and perhaps spoiled

Draws and identifies what they've drawn

Stacks block towers of six blocks or more

Recognizes basic shapes and point them out elsewhere

Their first sentence is around 18 months

Mastery of language shows up influence use of words that are appropriate and deliberate

Curious about their environment, seeking to identify letters at an early age

And early interest in the meanings of words and in reproducing letters

Excellent information processing abilities can be noted

Advanced working memory

Reaching the stages of sitting, standing, and walking early

They appear very early to be into everything, eager, and curious

They prefer a complex games, and electoral challenges, and brainteasers

They are always ready to experiment and innovate and are creative

They take an interest in life and earth sciences, astronomy, metaphysics, and books

Preschoolers

Ages 2 to 3 years

Excellent attention for a favorite TV or videos

Shows tremendous interest in printing letters and numbers

Will catch your mistakes, hold you to your word, and not forget promises or changes of plans

Frustrated with own lack of ability, seems to obsess on some things

People outside the family start to comment on how smart your child is

Has trouble playing with other children same age, prefers adults are much older children but is not a lot of fun for them because they are still too immature

Throws fits her tantrums especially when not able to do something his or her own way to completion

Can play with games, puzzles and toys that state and age range twice their own or more

Early reading

Most tantrums precipitated by lack of adult respect or understanding, child is more likely to cooperate then simply comply with adult demands

Highly competitive

Ages 4 to 5 years

May have asynchrony between their advanced understanding of concepts and their actual body capabilities

Too much focus on academics at this age can impact their abilities to fine-tune their motor skills

They have a highly active imagination which can rapidly become a source of anxiety

Many start reading simple books and then chapter books spontaneously before they are five

Interested in mature subjects but can be frightened by their own lack of perspective

Preschoolers

(Ages 4-5 continued)

Intuitive grasp of numerical concepts and mathematical reasoning, can effectively compete with older children and adults and board and card games

May start to question the meaning of life, their own worth, etc.

Huge vocabulary, huge memory for facts, events, and information

Increasing facility with computers and keyboarding, video games

Obvious abstract reasoning ability, love of concepts and theorizing, philosophical and speculative

Great need to engage others in meaningful and intelligent conversation about the things that interest them

A greater duration of REM sleep than other children

A higher frequency of eye movement during REM sleep

A large working memory capacity

Ability to screen out unsuitable information to avoid disturbance by distractors

A faster processing speed on cognitive problem-solving tasks

A high level of emotional sensitivity, which allows for the early development of values, empathy, and responsibility

A strong concern for others and their feelings

May also have intra-and interpersonal conflict due to being sensitive

May struggle with feelings of being different, I need for recognition, and impatience with others

More likely to respond to complex humor like riddles and verbal associations

Can powers of observation

Ability to generalize concepts

Ability to put together a 20 piece puzzle before age 3

Early interest in time – clocks, calendars

Imaginary playmates

Made in the USA
Middletown, DE
11 September 2021